The Sacred Feminine

Searching for the Hidden Face of God.

Joseph Lumpkin

The Sacred Feminine: Searching for the Hidden Face of God

By Joseph Lumpkin

Copyright © 2011

All rights reserved.

Printed in the United States of America. No part of this book may be used or reproduced in any manner whatsoever without written permission except in the case of brief quotations embodied in critical articles and reviews.

All people and facts in this book are factious. Any resemblance to real people or facts is coincidental.

Fifth Estate Publishers,

Post Office Box 116, Blountsville, AL 35031.

First Printing 2011

Cover art by

Printed on acid-free paper

Library of Congress Control No: 2011933216

ISBN: 9781936533138

Fifth Estate

2011

Preface

The purpose of this book is to expand and balance our view of God. Through thousands of years of interpreting the Bible through the lens of changing societies and varying regard to females and feminine qualities, the concept of God has become more and more male to the exclusion of God's female side of wisdom, mercy, grace, and nurture.

This book should not an any way be construed as an impetus toward a gender neutral Bible or religion, but instead it is an attempt to rediscover the truth and expand our understanding of the complete and perfect master we have for millennia called our Father God. If God is our creator and is all good things, then God is both our father and our mother.

After thousands of years of distortion, it is now time to look at both sides of God.

Part One

In The Beginning...

The search for the Sacred Feminine is the search taking place within each of us. It is a search for the recognition, integration, and balance of our masculine and feminine attributes. The individual need to find and integrate these energies is reflected in our evolving theologies. Society's conservative norms are mirrored in our beliefs. Theology is the slowly-moving reflection of our psychological journey expressed through our religion.

If there is a Sacred Masculine, there must also be a Sacred Feminine. General attributes of male and female are not universally clearly defined and vary from one society to another. The definitions as to what makes up the male and female attributes are general and are taken from socially accepted norms. It should be clear, however, that each of us has a mixture of both male and female attributes.

In general, male attributes are power, physical strength, law, justice, and will. Female attributes are wisdom, compassion, creation, grace, and nurturing. Spiritually, the male attributes of law and power (punitiveness) must be balanced with the female attributes of grace and mercy (forgiveness). Balance is paramount, because power is destructive without wisdom. The strength to destroy must be balanced with a creative force. The force of will crushes others without the reflex to also nurture and protect. As we try to find, understand, and balance the male and female parts of God, we should also seek this balance within ourselves.

How and why the two sexes came into existence is recounted in the Bible. The accepted biblical account of creation in the book of Genesis has God creating the two sexes. Other Christian and Jewish sects reinterpret the creation story in various ways. Certain mystical Jewish communities have another way of looking at the story of creation, which is not accepted by orthodox Christianity:

There was a single, complete, perfect Spirit (the All), that had the wish to experience itself in individualization, in a "Love" relationship to see all aspects of love as the Lover, the Beloved, and Love Itself.

In order to see and experience love from all perspectives, the Spirit (the All) differentiated Itself into two parts. It remained it's Infinite Self and it created, from Itself, a being just like Itself in all ways, except for being finite. This "being" is known in Christianity as the Holy Spirit, which in the Old Testament, resided in particular places, like the Temple, and was called "The Spirit of God", "Ruak", and "Shikhina". However, these are three different names for the same attributes and energy.

These two, the Spirit and the All, related in Bliss, the relationship polarizing the Infinite into will and power of The Father, and the Finite into wisdom, creation, and nurturing of The Holy Spirit. The former is defined spiritually as the divine or Sacred Masculine and the latter the divine or Sacred Feminine. The offspring of their Blissful interactions was the Only Begotten, Love Itself, Christ, and all else that was created was created in the same pattern of Blissful interactions between Will and Power and Intelligence and Wisdom, through the Son, the Logos (the Living Word).

All of creation exists from this interaction - as Father and Mother energies giving birth. In Judaism this spiral of creation is called the Tree of Life. In Christianity, the creation is the Body of Christ – created by the Logos.

It is said that God created everything in the first six days. Everything must also include the souls of those who would be born. Since our spiritual creation, we have communed with our perfect, complete God. Once, we knew the bliss of unity and communion between God and ourselves. On earth, as Adam and Eve, we knew the fullness of the whole expression of God within us. We communed with God and we communed in peace and understanding with each other, but we fell from grace and lost unity with our creator. Mankind now exists as incomplete and unbalanced men and women, an expression of our fall from grace. Our outer and inner beings now exist cut off from each other and are veiled to the Kingdom within, separated from God and our spiritual self. Over time, in our corrupt world, power overwhelmed wisdom and our idea of God began to warp into an unbalanced masculine view, leaving behind the female part of ourselves and our God.

The term, Sacred Feminine, does not refer to a specific female or deity, but to the idea of the balance of the feminine attributes and energies with the ubiquitous male energy within a particular theology. In this case, we will discuss the Sacred Feminine within the Judeo-Christian framework.

From the time of the ancient Jews, man has struggled with the inability to understand and balance the manifold attributes of God. In a society built upon war and survival, the world and our view of God must have taken on a harsh tone. It is easy to simply assume that a male-driven theology would only have male attributes, and certainly, this monocular approach had its effect, but that is only part of the story. There was also love, family, the flowing poetry of King David, and the passionate prose of Solomon. To understand the muting of the feminine force within Judaism and later within Christianity, one must delve back into a history that, until recently, was hidden, if not occluded.

Religions do not usually spring into existence and remain stable or stagnant. Religions evolve and morph, changing with the social pressures, absorbing various beliefs, costumes, and practices from converts and those around whom the practitioners live. So it was with Judaism.

Scholars have long wondered why the God of the Old Testament had two names, El, usually translated as God, and Yahweh (Jehovah), usually translated as Lord. Moreover, the two personas seem to have different personalities. This is seen quite clearly in the distinct change between the God of the Pentateuch and the God of the Gospels. Notice I pointed to the God of the Gospels and not the New Testament, since in the beginning of these books Jesus had not been born and had not died, forming the new covenant of the New Testament. Up until the sacrifice, we can still view everything through the eyes and laws of the Old Testament.

Even though we are taught that Judaism was always a monotheistic religion, this was not the case. The evolution of Judaism into its current form gives us insight into the first steps away from the balance between male and female energies and attributes contained within one God.

Judaism was formed in part by the pressures of the mingling of peoples and customs around Canaan, also called the Ugarit region.

The ancient Canaanite city-state of Ugarit is of utmost importance for those who study the Old Testament. Writings found there have aided greatly in our understanding of the meaning of various Biblical passages, as well as in deciphering difficult Hebrew words. Ugarit was at its height around the 12th century BCE. This was the period corresponding with the entry of Israel into Canaan.

The people of this region worshiped a god called, "El." The wife of El was Ashtoreth, whose title was, "The Queen of Heaven." Ugaritic polytheism is made up of a divine council or assembly. This assembly is populated by the divine family, made up of the head god, his wife, and their offspring. The chief god, El, and his wife, Ashtoreth, are said to have produced seventy divine children, some of whose names may be familiar as they include Baal, Astarte, Anat, Resheph, the sun-goddess Shapshu, and the moon-god Yerak. Some sources also list the name, Yah, or Yahweh. These children came to be called, "the stars of El." Below the divine counsel are the helpers of the divine household. Kothar wa-Hasis was the head of these helpers. It is thought the servants or helpers of the divine household came to be known as the entities the Bible calls "angels". The word for angel means messenger and these helpers were in fact, messenger-gods. Ashtoreth would become Asherah in the Israelites worship.

In the earliest stages of this religion, Yahweh appears to be simply one of these seventy children, each of whom was the patron deity of the seventy nations. We see this idea of city-state having patron gods brought into the ancient Greek religions as well. The idea also appears in the Dead Sea Scrolls reading and the Septuagint translation of Deuteronomy 32:8.

Deuteronomy 32:8-9
Douay-Rheims 1899 American Edition (DRA)

8) When the Most High divided the nations: when he separated the sons of Adam, he appointed the bounds of people according to the number of the children of Israel
9) And his people Jacob became the portion of the Lord, Israel was the line of his inheritance.

Some sources, including the Masoretic Text; Dead Sea Scrolls (see also Septuagint) renders "children of Israel" as *"sons of God."*

As the patriarch, El, had divided the land, each member of the divine family received a nation of his own: Israel is the portion of Yahweh. The statement, "according to the number of the children of Israel" is thought to include the seventy children.

Psalm 82 also presents the god, El, presiding over a divine assembly at which Yahweh stands up and makes his accusation against the other gods.

Psalm 82
Amplified Bible (AMP)

A Psalm of Asaph.
1) GOD stands in the assembly [of the representatives] of God; in the midst of the magistrates or judges He gives judgment [as] among the gods.
2) How long will you [magistrates or judges] judge unjustly and show partiality to the wicked? Selah [pause, and calmly think of that]!
3) Do justice to the weak (poor) and fatherless; maintain the rights of the afflicted and needy.
4) Deliver the poor and needy; rescue them out of the hand of the wicked.
5) [The magistrates and judges] know not, neither will they understand; they walk on in the darkness [of complacent satisfaction]; all the foundations of the earth [the fundamental principles upon which rests the administration of justice] are shaking.
6) I said, You are gods [since you judge on My behalf, as My representatives]; indeed, all of you are children of the Most High.

7) But you shall die as men and fall as one of the princes.

8) Arise, O God, judge the earth! For to You belong all the nations.

Whether Yahweh was the son of El in the beginning of the mythos or not, at some time in the 8th century BCE, the names and deities begin to merge and be identified as one. Where El was a patriarchal and punitive God, Yahweh tended to interact with mankind. In the story of Abraham, as he rejects his father's god and is called into communion with the "one true God", we see this merging. This can be seen in Genesis 14, where Abraham interacts with Melchizedek, a priest of El Elyon, and Abraham verbally equates Yahweh with El Elyon. Remember, as a general rule, in our Bible "El" is translated as "God" (Elyon means the highest or the most high) and "Yahweh" is translated as "Lord."

Genesis 14
Amplified Bible (AMP)

17) After his [Abram's] return from the defeat and slaying of Chedorlaomer and the kings who were with him, the king of Sodom went out to meet him at the Valley of Shaveh, that is, the King's Valley.

18) Melchizedek, king of Salem [later called Jerusalem] brought out bread and wine [for their nourishment]; he was the priest of God Most High,

19) And he blessed him and said, Blessed (favored with blessings, made blissful, joyful) be Abram by God Most High, Possessor and Maker of heaven and earth,

20) And blessed, praised, and glorified be God Most High, Who has given your foes into your hand! And [Abram] gave him a tenth of all [he had taken].

21) And the king of Sodom said to Abram, "Give me the persons and keep the goods for yourself."

22) But Abram said to the king of Sodom, "I have lifted up my hand and sworn to **the Lord, God Most High**, the Possessor and Maker of heaven and earth,

23) That I would not take a thread or a shoelace or anything that is yours, lest you should say, I have made Abram rich."

Because the two identities were merging into one, the deity now known as Yahweh-El was the husband of the goddess, Asherah, also known as the "Queen of Heaven."

Evidently, this is the situation represented by the biblical condemnations of her cult symbol in the Jerusalem temple and in the inscriptions mentioned above. In this form, the religious devotion to Yahweh casts him in the role of the Divine King ruling over all the other deities. This religious outlook appears, for example, in Psalm 29:2, where the "sons of God", or really divine sons or children, are called upon to worship Yahweh, the Divine King.

Psalm 29
Amplified Bible (AMP)

A Psalm of David.

1) ASCRIBE to the Lord, O sons of the mighty, ascribe to the Lord glory and strength.

2) Give to the Lord the glory due to His name; worship the Lord in the beauty of holiness or in holy array.

3) The voice of the Lord is upon the waters; the God of glory thunders; the Lord is upon many (great) waters.

4) The voice of the Lord is powerful; the voice of the Lord is full of majesty.

5) The voice of the Lord breaks the cedars; yes, the Lord breaks in pieces the cedars of Lebanon.

6) He makes them also to skip like a calf; Lebanon and Sirion (Mount Hermon) like a young, wild ox.

7) The voice of the Lord splits and flashes forth forked lightning.

8) The voice of the Lord makes the wilderness tremble; the Lord shakes the Wilderness of Kadesh.

9) The voice of the Lord makes the hinds bring forth their young, and His voice strips bare the forests, while in His temple everyone is saying, Glory!

10) The Lord sat as King over the deluge; the Lord [still] sits as King [and] forever!

11) The Lord will give [unyielding and impenetrable] strength to His people; the Lord will bless His people with peace.

The temple, which revealed various expressions of polytheism such as the lesser gods in the forms of cherubim and seraphim, assumed and demonstrated that this place was Yahweh's palace which was populated by those under his power. The other gods became mere expressions of Yahweh's power, and the divine messengers became understood as little more than minor divine beings expressive of Yahweh's power. The idea of angels and demons began to emerge as lesser beings controlled by the One True God and the head god became the godhead of today.

As religion tends to mimic society over time, the idea of a divine family became less important and the family-to-family influence of the Canaanites gave way to a new paradigm. Family lineages were changed or destroyed in the eighth century with major social upheaval and Assyrian incursions. Before then, entire families were held accountable for the acts of a single member, but in the seventh and sixth centuries, we begin to see expressions of individual identity.

Deuteronomy 26:16

16) This day the Lord your God has commanded you to do these statutes and ordinances. Therefore you shall keep and do them with all your [mind and] heart and with all your being.

17) You have [openly] declared the Lord this day to be your God, [pledging] to walk in His ways, to keep His statutes and His commandments and His precepts, and to hearken to His voice.

18) And the Lord has declared this day that you are His peculiar people as He promised you, and you are to keep all His commandments;

19) And He will make you high above all nations which He has made, in praise and in fame and in honor, and that you shall be a holy people to the Lord your God, as He has spoken.

With the emergence of individual accountability came the idea that an individual deity was accountable for the cosmos. The rise of the individual as a social unit provided the rise of a single god rather than a divine family.

Still, some of the people held on to the belief that God had a wife. There was a "Queen of Heaven," even though the orthodox belief had changed. The change is well documented in the exact phrasing within the Ten Commandments.

Exodus 20:2-17 NKJV

"I am the Lord your God, who brought you out of the land of Egypt, out of the house of bondage. You shall have no other gods before Me."

The passage is an acknowledgement that there were other gods. In our western society, which is so different than the polytheistic societies of the time, we have learned to equate this passage as a warning against having any item or desire, such as money or success, come before God, but this interpretation is a modern one and does not fit the time or society of the text.

Another example of the implication of the acknowledgement of multiple gods is Exodus 15:

Exodus 15
Amplified Bible (AMP)

1) Then Moses and the Israelites sang this song to the Lord, saying, I will sing to the Lord, for He has triumphed gloriously; the horse and his rider or its chariot has He thrown into the sea.

2) The Lord is my Strength and my Song, and He has become my Salvation; this is my God, and I will praise Him, my father's God, and I will exalt Him.

3) The Lord is a Man of War; the Lord is His name.

4) Pharaoh's chariots and his host has He cast into the sea; his chosen captains also are sunk in the Red Sea.

5) The floods cover them; they sank in the depths [clad in mail] like a stone.

6) Your right hand, O Lord, is glorious in power; Your right hand, O Lord, shatters the enemy.

7) In the greatness of Your majesty You overthrow those rising against You. You send forth Your fury; it consumes them like stubble.

8) With the blast of Your nostrils the waters piled up, the floods stood fixed in a heap, the deeps congealed in the heart of the sea.

9) The enemy said, I will pursue, I will overtake, I will divide the spoil; my desire shall be satisfied upon them; I will draw my sword, my hand shall destroy them.

10) You [Lord] blew with Your wind, the sea covered them; [clad in mail] they sank as lead in the mighty waters.

11) Who is like You, O Lord, among the gods? Who is like You, glorious in holiness, awesome in splendor, doing wonders?

The question, "Who is like You, O Lord, among the gods?" assumes there are other gods and Yahweh is mightier than them all.

In the book of Jeremiah, we see one of these gods called out by name. It is the title given to the wife of God. Indeed, the people held this goddess in such high regard that the number and significance of the objects of veneration to her cannot be denied. So many pillar figurines have been excavated in Judah that they are now re-garded as "a characteristic expression of piety" for those who worship El and his consort.

Part Two

The Sacred Feminine Emerges

Figurines or statuettes found in great numbers in various archeological excavations all depict a female naked to the waist with prominent, unusually large breasts, which she cups with her hands. These figurines are thought to be household shrines. The figurines get their name from the fact that the lower part, which looks like a long, flared skirt, is usually described as a pillar or a pedestal, even as "pole like"

In the past twenty-five years, a number of scholars have suggested that the pillar figurines may depict the goddess Asherah statuette as like a pole, a description which suggests that they interpret the biblical "asherahs" as poles and therefore, understand the figurines as "small clay counterparts of the larger wooden Asherah poles which were set up by implanting them in the ground."

It seems likely that, during the Israelite Monarchy, Ashtoreth was no longer associated with Canaanite worship, but was now Asherah and was part of the Israelite's official religion as the consort of the Israelite god. Relatively recently, startling archaeological discoveries in modern Israel have confirmed this.

Archeological excavations in the heartland of Judah, and in the northern Sinai revealed several blessing inscriptions from the sites contain a controversial phrase possibly to be translated as "Yahweh and his Asherah." Even more exciting are drawings that accompany the inscriptions, especially those from the Sinai site.

The Sinai sketches appear on several pieces of pottery from two large jars found in a strange structure in the northern Sinai. One of the accompanying inscriptions reads: "I bless you by Yahweh of Samaria and his [/its] Asherah," while the two others use the formula: "I bless you by Yahweh of Teman (the South) and his [/its] Asherah".

We see traces in the Bible of Asherah worship when King Solomon brought the practice to Jerusalem. Solomon "loved YHVH", but "also burned incense in high places". This refers to the practice of burning incense to Asherah whose statues were always placed in high areas, on hilltops, etc. Solomon married the daughter of Pharaoh, a Sidonian Princess, and a Hittite Princess, and daughters of the ruling elite of Moab, Ammonites, and Edomites. Many of these women came from the old pagan religions that worshipped Asharah, also known by some as Ishtar. To appease his wives, Solomon allowed the idols to be placed in the Holy of Holies next to the Ark of the Covenant.

The worship of Asharah ended in the Kingdom of Israel, at least, when the Assyrians sacked it in 721 BCE. There was a remnant of the Israelites who still remained behind in Samaria and tried to continue the Asherah worship along with the worship of YHVH.

It was the practice of the day that when a people were conquered, they would take up the religion of the victors, believing the gods of those who conquered them must be more powerful than their god. This was not the case when Israel was sacked. Instead, the Israelites held fast to their belief that they alone were the chosen people of God. The question then became, "Why is our God angry with us that he would allow us to be destroyed?" For the answer they turned back to the Ten Commandments and the Law. This was the turning point where the Jewish people became monotheistic. A ground swell arose against the worship of the consort of God, and she was banished from the nation, leaving a void of the Sacred Feminine in the psyche of the people. After all, the total of all female attributes and energy was tied up in the fertility and mother goddess, the queen of heaven, who was no longer welcome.

Jeremiah 7
Amplified Bible (AMP)

15) And I will cast you out of My sight, as I have cast out all your brethren, even the whole posterity of Ephraim.

16) Therefore do not pray for this people [of Judah] or lift up a cry or entreaty for them or make intercession to Me, for I will not listen to or hear you.

17) Do you not see what they are doing in the cities of Judah and in the streets of Jerusalem?

18) The children gather wood, the fathers kindle the fire, and the women knead the dough, to make cakes for the queen of heaven; and they pour out drink offerings to other gods, that they may provoke Me to anger!

Jeremiah 44
Amplified Bible (AMP)

15) Then all the men who knew that their wives were burning incense to other gods, and all the women who stood by a great assembly, even all the people who dwelt in Pathros in the land of Egypt, answered Jeremiah:

16) "As for the word that you have spoken to us in the name of the Lord, we will not listen to or obey you.

17) But we will certainly perform every word of the vows we have made: to burn incense to the queen of heaven and to pour out drink offerings to her as we have done, we and our fathers, our kings and our princes - in the cities of Judah and in the streets of Jerusalem; for then we had plenty of food and were well off and prosperous and saw no evil.

18) But since we stopped burning incense to the queen of heaven and pouring out drink offerings to her, we have lacked everything and have been consumed by the sword and by famine."

19) [And the wives said] "When we burned incense to the queen of heaven and poured out drink offerings to her, did we make cakes [in the shape of a star] to represent and honor her and pour out drink offerings to her without [the knowledge and approval of] our husbands?"

20) Then Jeremiah said to all the people to the men and to the women and to all the people who had given him that answer.

21) "The incense that you burned in the cities of Judah and in the streets of Jerusalem, you and your fathers, your kings and your princes, and the people of the land, did not the Lord [earnestly] remember [your idolatrous wickedness] and did it not come into His mind?

22) The Lord could no longer endure the evil of your doings and the abominations which you have committed; because of them therefore has your land become a desolation and an [astonishing] waste and a curse, without inhabitants, as it is this day.

23) Because you have burned incense [to idols] and because you have sinned against the Lord and have not obeyed the voice of the Lord or walked in His law and in His statutes and in His testimonies, therefore this evil has fallen upon you, as it is this day."

It is difficult to know why the void of the feminine was not filled with the principles the people once understood, just as it is difficult to know why the people could not fully conceive of such an abstract form of God as a spirit containing both male and female energies. Perhaps Genesis, being written around the 5th or 6th centuries BCE, was articulating an understanding of what had been worked out after hundreds of years of polytheism. Many parts of the Old Testament were written after the decision to adopt monotheism, but before the completion of the transition.

Part Three

The Two Are Made One

They had the answer from the beginning. God, the true God, had evolved in the psyche of the writer or writers of the book of Genesis to include both male and female attributes. The people's ability to conceive of a God who could incorporate infinite male and female attributes within himself at the same time had expanded.

According to the Old Testament book of Genesis in Hebrew text, there was a balance of male and female forces within God from the beginning. Neither male nor female, both male and female, God showed the male energy of forming and shaping, as well as the female energy of nurturing and brooding. Although one may have a difficult time in distinguishing God the Spirit from the Spirit of God, the word for "spirit" is "ruach" and is a female word.

Genesis 1
Amplified Bible
  1) In the beginning God (prepared, formed, fashioned, and) created the heavens and the earth.
  2) The earth was without form and an empty waste, and darkness was upon the face of the very great deep. The Spirit of God was moving (hovering, brooding) over the face of the waters.

The Holy Spirit is the designated representation of the feminine principle. This idea is supported by the Hebrew word for "spirit". Jerome, the author of the Latin Vulgate knew this when he rendered the passage into Latin. He is quoted as saying:

"In the Gospel of the Hebrews that the Nazarenes read it says, 'Just now my mother, the Holy Spirit, took me.' Now, no one should be offended by this, because "spirit" in Hebrew is feminine, while in our language [Latin] it is masculine, and in Greek it is neuter. In divinity, however, there is no gender."

In Jerome's Commentary on Isaiah 11, an explanation contains a pointed observation. There was a tradition among a sect of Early Christians which believed that the Holy Spirit was our Lord's spiritual mother. Jerome comments that the Hebrew word for "spirit" (ruach or ruak) is feminine, meaning, that for the 1st Century Christians in the Aramaic world, the Holy Spirit was a feminine figure. This was likely because in the beginning, the converts to this new cult of Judaism, called Christianity, were mostly Jews. The gender was lost in the translation from the Hebrew into the Greek, rendering it neuter, and then it was changed to a masculine gender when it was translated from the Greek into the Latin.

The Bible in Genesis describes a male/female God with male creating and female brooding. But, man could not hold onto that unfamiliar concept and the primitive Jews chose to take up the

Canaanite deities of the God, El and his wife, Asherah. But, she was simply a fertility goddess.

Although the balance of male and female energies were presented in Genesis from the outset, primitive man was not ready to accept or understand the spiritual truth of balance. Instead, mankind had to evolve spiritually over thousands of years until they were ready to resume the search for the Sacred Feminine. This time, it was within their one true God. Monotheism does not easily reveal the dualism of male and female forces.

Even today, the churches continue to struggle with the fact that God is at once male and female. God is neither. God is both. God is all.

Possibly, if we better understood the original language and context of the time, the church would not have gone so far astray. The word used for the station of women in conjunction with men is "helpmeet."

The truth has been there in the Bible all along. Let us look closely at the words used regarding the place of woman in regards to man. The word used is "Helpmeet."

HELP

Strong's # 5828 (**Hebrew - ezer**) aid: - help *Strong's* Root # 5826 (Hebrew - azar) azar - prime root: to surround, i.e., protect or aid: help, succor
Heinrich Friedrich Wilhelm Gesenius (1786–1842), noted author of the first Hebrew lexicon, adds that the primary idea lies in girding, surrounding, hence defending

MEET

(**Hebrew - *kenegdo***) corresponding to, counterpart to, equal to matching

The traditional teaching for the woman as help (meet) is that of assistant or helper subservient to the one being helped. This definition would appear to line up with Strong's definition of the word. However, if you look at the context of every other use of the word *ezer* in the scripture, you will see that *ezer* refers to either God or military allies. In all other cases the one giving the help is superior to the one receiving the help. Adding *kenegdo* (meet) modifies the meaning to that of equal rather than superior status

Dr. Susan Hyatt gives the following definition from her book *In the Spirit We're Equal:* "Re: Hebrew *ezer kenegdo*. In Genesis 2:18, the word "Helpmeet " does not occur. The Hebrew expression *ezer kenegdo* appears meaning, "one who is the same as the other and who surrounds, protects, aids, helps, supports." There is no indication of inferiority or of a secondary position in a hierarchical separation of the male and female "spheres" of responsibility, authority, or social position.

The word *ezer* is used twice in the Old Testament to refer to the female and 14 times to refer to God. For example, in the Psalms when David says, "The Lord is my Helper," he uses the word *ezer*."

Usages of *'ezer* in the Old Testament show that in most cases God is an 'ezer to human beings, which calls to question if the word "helper" is a valid interpretation of *'ezer* in any instance it is used. "Evidence indicates that the word *'ezer* originally had two roots, each beginning with different guttural sounds. One meant "power" and the other "strength." As time passed, the two guttural sounds merged, but the meanings remained the same. The article below by William Sulik explains this point quite well. He references R. David Freedman and Biblical Archaeology Review 9 [1983]: (56-58).

"She was to be his "helper". At least, that is how most of the translations have interpreted this word. A sample of the translations reads as follows:

'I shall make a helper fit for him' (RSV); 'I will make a fitting helper for him' (New Jewish Publication Society); 'I will make an aid fit for him' (AB); 'I will make him a helpmate' (JB); 'I will make a suitable partner for him' (NAB); 'I will make him a helper comparable to him' (NKJV).

[Source: *Hard Sayings of the Bible* by Walter C. Kaiser, Peter H. Davids, F. F. Bruce, and Manfred Brauch]

However, the customary translation of the two words `*ezer kenegdo* as "helper fit" is almost certainly wrong. Recently R. David Freedman has pointed out that the Hebrew word *ezer* is a combination of two roots: `-z-r, meaning "to rescue, to save," and g-z-r, meaning "to be strong." The difference between the two is the first letter in the Hebrew language.

Today, that letter is silent in the Hebrew; but in ancient times, it was a guttural sound formed in the back of the throat. The "g" was a *ghayyin*, and it came to use the same Hebrew symbol as the other sound, `*ayin*. But the fact that they were pronounced differently is clear from such names of places which preserve the "g" sound, such as Gaza or Gomorrah. Some Semitic languages distinguished between these two signs and others did not. For example, Ugaritic did make a distinction between the `*ayin* and the *ghayyin*; Hebrew did not. (R. David Freedman, "*Woman, a Power Equal to a Man*,"

Biblical Archaeology Review 9 [1983]: 56-58).

It would appear that sometime around 1500 BCE, these two signs began to be represented by one sign in Phoenician. Consequently, the two "phonemes" merged into one "grapheme." What had been two different roots merged into one, much as in English the one word "fast" can refer to a person's speed, abstinence from food, his or her slyness in a "fast deal," or the adamant way in which someone holds "fast" to positions. The noun `ezer occurs twenty-one times in the Old Testament. In many of the passages, it is used in parallelism to words that clearly denote strength or power. Some examples of this are:

"There is none like the God of Jeshurun, The Rider of the Heavens in your strength (`-z-r), and on the clouds in his majesty."

(Deut.33:26 [source author's translation])
"Blessed are you, O Israel! Who is like you, a people saved by the Lord? He is the shield of your strength (`-z-r) and the sword of your majesty." (Deut. 33:29, [source author's translation]

The case begins to build for the surety that `ezer means "strength" or "power" whenever it is used in parallelism with words for majesty or other words for power such as `oz or `uzzo. In fact, the presence of two names for one king, Azariah and Uzziah, both referring to God's strength, makes it abundantly clear that the root `ezer` meaning "strength" was known in Hebrew.

Therefore, could we conclude that Genesis 2:18 be translated as, "I will make a power [or strength] corresponding to man."   Freedman even suggests, on the basis of later Hebrew, that the second word in the Hebrew expression found in this verse should be rendered "equal to him." If so, then God makes a woman fully his equal and fully his match for the man. In this way, the man's loneliness is assuaged.

The same line of reasoning occurs with the apostle Paul, who urged in 1 Corinthians 11:10, "For this reason, a woman must have power [or authority] on her head [that is to say, invested in her]."

This line of reasoning, which stresses full equality, is continued in Genesis 2:23 where Adam says of Eve, "This is now bone of my bones and flesh of my flesh; she shall be called 'woman,' for she was taken out of man." The idiomatic sense of this phrase, "bone of my bones", is a "very close relative" to "one of us" or, in effect, "our equal."

The woman was never meant to be an assistant or "helpmate" to the man. The word "mate" slipped into English since it was so close to the Old English word "meet," which means "fit to" or "corresponding to" the man which comes from the   phrase   that   likely   means   "equal   to."

What God had intended, then, was to make a "power" or "strength" for the man who would in every way "correspond to him", or even "be his equal." The closest word connecting the corporeal station of "helpmeet" to the spiritual world within the Godhead is the word that explains the female attributes and energies within God. That word is "Ruach," also spelled "Ruak," since transliteration from Hebrew is not precise. The spirit of God, Ruach, is a female word. Ruach broods and nurtures. She "mothers." To this day, few people, Jew or Christian, have understood this. Others continue to view the deities as two separate entities, just as Yahweh and His consort.

Let us consider a word or two and the various ways the translators have decided to render the words. We will begin with the Hebrew word, "*Chayil.*"

Virtuous = Strong's #2428 (*chayil*) wealth, virtue, valor, strength, might, power.

Before we precede, it must be understood that Hebrew has a reasonably small lexicon. Words are interpreted according to context. The same form may be used as a noun, a verb, an adjective, or an adverb.

Chayil occurs 242 times in the Old Testament. It is translated "army" and "war" 58 times; "host" and "forces" 43 times; "might" or "power" 16 times; "goods," "riches," "substance" and "wealth" in all 31 times; "band of soldiers," "band of men," "company," and "train" once each"; "activity" once; "valor" 28 times; "strength" 11 times: these are all noun forms. The word is often translated as an adjective or adverb.

It is translated "valiant" and "valiantly" 35 times; "strong" 6 times; "able" 4 times; "worthily" once, and "worthy" once. One can see a pattern to the translations of the word. All choices connote power, war, ability, and substance. However, these are the translations of the word only when the translators saw that the word applied to a male, or the actions or results of actions enacted by a man or by men.

In the four instances in which the word is used in describing a woman, the word seems to be rendered as if it were not the same word. In the four cases relating to women, the word is translated differently, and the choices of the words used to rendered *Chayil* into English shows a gender bias.

Ruth, the Moabitess, was a woman of courage, loyalty, and decisiveness. In her loyalty to her dead husband's mother, she refused to leave her mother-in-law and re-marry in her own land, but was inalterably determined to accompany her mother-in-law to a foreign land. There, in an unknown city she committed herself to the task of keeping them both from starvation. She labored tirelessly. Boaz, recognizing her traits would later say to her: "All the city of my people doth know that thou art a woman of *cha-yil*," (Ruth 3:11). The Septuagint rendered the Hebrew word, *Chayil*, into Greek as follows, "Thou art a woman of power" (dunamis).

In the last chapter of Proverbs, there is a description of an ideal wife, whose "price is far above rubies. Here are some of her characteristics: "She is like the merchants' ships, she brings her food from afar." "She considers a field and buys it." "She girds her loins with strength, and strengthens her arms." "Strength and honor are her clothing." The is obviously a woman of determination, strength, and will. This is the kind of woman a mother would choose to marry her son. The translators wrote: "Who can find a virtuous woman? "Virtue" is a moral quality, but does not capture the impressive strength of a women who works day and night in many areas of life and is a success in them all, as the Proverb indicated about this woman. The word used for "Virtue" is the Hebrew word, "*Chayil*." She is a "Mighty" woman.

The ideal woman is summed up in the 29th verse, in the words: "Many daughters have done *cha-yil*, but thou excel them all. "Worthily," "valiantly," are the only translations that we have in any other part of the Bible for this word where it is applied to a man, but here, the word is translated "virtuously" to the female.

In Proverbs 12:4, the Hebrew text reads, "A woman of *cha-yil* is a crown to her husband." The translators render the English text as, "A virtuous woman is a crown to her husband." Again, Septuagint translates the word as a word for strength, power, might, valor, ability, uprightness, integrity.

To sum up the difference in word choices of the translation of "*Chayil*", let us look at the grouping of the examples below:

Ruth 3:11 And now my daughter, fear not, I will do to thee all that thou require; for all the city of my people know that thou art a virtuous *[chayil]* woman.

Proverbs 12:4 A virtuous *[chayil]* woman is a crown to her husband; but she that makes ashamed is as rottenness in his bones.

Proverbs 31:10 Who can find a virtuous *[chayil]* woman? For her price is far above rubies.

Proverbs 31:29 Many daughters have done virtuously *[chayil]* , but thou excel them all.

In **Ps. 18:32 and 39** the word *Chayil* is translated as strength.

Ps.18:32 It is God that girds me with strength *[chayil]*, and makes my way perfect.
vs. 39 For thou hast girded me with strength *[chayil]* unto the battle: thou hast subdued under me those that rose up against me.

The Torah Study for Reform Jews says, "From the time of creation, relationships between spouses have at times been adversarial."

In Genesis 2:18, God calls woman an *ezer kenegdo,* a "helper against him." The great commentator, Rashi, takes the term literally to make a wonderful point: "If he [Adam] is worthy, [she will be] a help *[ezer].* If he is not worthy [she will be] against him *[kenegdo]* for strife." This Jewish study also described man and woman facing each other with arms raised holding an arch between them, giving a beautiful picture of equal responsibility

Although a small number of Christian denominations have managed to re-capture some type of balance between male and female energy within the godhead, most have not.

An official publication of the LDS (Mormon) Church states:

"Our Father in heaven was once a man as we are now, capable of physical death. By obedience to eternal gospel principles, he progressed from one stage of life to another until he attained the state that we call exaltation or godhood. In such a condition, he and our mother in heaven were empowered to give birth to spirit children whose potential was equal to that of their heavenly parents. We are those spirit children." (Achieving a Celestial Marriage p 132)

The LDS (Mormon) Church offers courses in religion and supplies books and manuals from which to teach. In the 3rd chapter of the manual for a course entitled, *Doctrines of the Gospel,* that is part of an advanced course for the Religion 231 and 232, we find the church addresses the nature of God. Joseph Smith's "King Follett" sermon is cited as authoritative by this official Church publication along with a statement from Spencer W. Kimball, one of the earlier church prophets:

God made man in his own image and certainly he made woman in the image of his wife-partner (Spencer W. Kimball, The Teachings of Spencer W. Kimball, p.25).

Again we encounter the concept of the heavenly Mother, God's wife in heaven, and have the interesting assertion that women are made, not in the image of God, but in the image of God's wife-partner.

In the above quotes, we see the Church of Jesus Christ of Latter day Saints sought to fill the void of the divine or Sacred Feminine with an entity, who was the wife of God.

It is within the Christian Science Church, also called the Church of Christ Scientists, that the balance of a singular God containing all attributes of both male and female is encountered again after thousands of years.

In the church of Christ Scientists (Christian Science), God is hailed as "The Mother-Father God," vocalizing their held belief of the existence of attributes and energies of both male and female within the spirit of God.

Mary Baker Eddy defined God as "the all-knowing, all-seeing, all-acting, all-wise, all-loving, and eternal; Principle; Mind; Soul; Spirit; Truth; Love; all substance; intelligence" (Eddy 587). Very importantly, Mrs. Eddy throughout her writing also refers to God as the Father-Mother God.

Mary Baker Eddy was not the first one to perceive God as being both Father and Mother (Peel 91). Mother Ann Lee, a Shaker woman, was part of just one of many faiths that spoke of God as Mother. She wrote:

"As Father, God is the infinite Fountain of intelligence, and the Source of all power, "the Almighty and

terrible in majesty"; "the high and lofty one, that inhabiteth eternity, whose name is Holy, dwelling in the high and holy place"; and "a consuming fire." But as, Mother, "God is Love" and tenderness. If all the maternal affections of all the female or bearing spirits in animated nature were combined together, and then concentrated in one individual human female, that person would be put as the type or image of our Eternal Heavenly Mother." (Peel 28).

This matches the Christian Science understanding of God's motherly aspects and serves as a helpful illustration of the maternal nature of God as Mother. God as Father is a powerful being that offers intelligence and strength; yet there is something untouchable about Him. God as Mother can be seen as our earthly mothers, tender, nurturing, maternal, and approachable.

Mary Baker Eddy produced an interpretation of the Lord's Prayer based on her understanding of the balance of male and female elements within the Godhead.

Lord's Prayer with Spiritual Interpretation by Mary Baker Eddy
Our Father which art in heaven,
Our Father-Mother God, all-harmonious,
Hallowed be Thy name.
Adorable One.
Thy kingdom come.
Thy kingdom is come; Thou art ever-present.

Thy will be done in earth, as it is in heaven.
Enable us to know – as in heaven, so on earth – God is omnipotent, supreme.
Give us this day our daily bread;
Give us grace for today; feed the famished affections;
And forgive us our debts, as we forgive our debtors.
And Love is reflected in love;
And lead us not into temptation, but deliver us from evil;
And God leadeth us not into temptation, but delivereth us from sin, disease, and death.
For Thine is the kingdom, and the power, and the glory, forever.
For God is infinite, all-power, all Life, Truth, Love, over all, and All.

Part Four

Defining
The Sacred Feminine

Having seen some of the attempts of the modern churches to understand and rectify the lack of recognition or understanding of the Sacred Feminine, it is necessary to ask, "What happened to the Sacred Feminine of Genesis? What initiated the lack of recognition or denial of the female side of God?"

The feminine side of God was erased with the change of language from the Hebrew feminine word "Ruak" into the Greek word "Pneuma" and into the Latin word "Spiritus". Both words, Spiritus and Pneuma mean "breath", but the word used in Latin is a masculine word and in Greek the word has no gender at all. Thus the feminine side of God simply disappeared into a linguistic void and was forgotten; never to be recognized for her nurturing and brooding nature until centuries later. Since the church was almost completely controlled by men at the time, they either did not notice or they did not care that the feminine spirit of God vanished and was replaced with a translation that rendered the spirit of God either neuter or masculine.

Although it is understood that God is a singular being, our psyches still call out for some manifestation of the female force. We long for a mother as well and a father. We search the Bible for the Sacred Feminine. In its pages we find no less than three distinct feminine archetypal forms within God: Ruak, Shikina, and Sophia (Wisdom).

In the pages of the New Testament and the teaching of the Catholic Church, we find the Sacred Feminine exemplified in the persons of Mary Magdalene and Mary, the mother of Jesus.

Let us first look at the feminine forces of Ruak, Shikhinah, and Sophia (Wisdom).

Ruak, Ruach, or Rawach:
We have already seen that Ruak was the spirit that hovered and brooded over the earth like a mother hen broods over her chicks. In the Ten Commandments, we are taught to "honor your father and your mother" and that doing so would make "your days long upon the land which Yahweh your God is giving you." There seems to be no obvious connection in the temporal sense, except that by not honoring your parents you could be stoned. However, if Yahweh is actually speaking of our spiritual father and mother, that is Yahweh and His Holy Spirit, then it all makes sense. Yahweh is the Creator, Provider, Protector, and ultimate Authority. These are all "male" traits. Ruak Qodesh or Holy Spirit is the maternal aspect of God. She is the Caregiver, Counselor, and Comforter.

Shekinah , Shechinah, Shekhina, or Shechina.

In the Hebrew language this word   means the glory or radiance of God. The Glory of God rests or resides in his house or Tabernacle amongst his people. Thus, the word is derived from the Hebrew word 'sakan', which means 'to dwell'.

The Shekhina is defined, in traditional Jewish writings, as the "female aspect of God." It is part of the feminine "presence" of the infinite God in the world. She is introduced in early rabbinical commentaries as the "immanence" or "indwelling" of the living God. Her purpose is to animate or impart life force. She is certainly not the 'Canaanite' Mother Goddess, Asherah. Around 622 BCE, King Josiah removed the Asherah from the Jerusalem temple and destroyed the shrines.

While she does not appear by name in the five books of Moses, her presence is seen in interpreting the text. For example, when Moses encounters the burning bush, he is told to remove his shoes and prepare himself to receive the Shekhina.

A Talmudic verse said: "Let them make Me a sanctuary that I may dwell (*ve'shakhanti*) among them."   In a later version, the translation said, "Let them make Me a Sanctuary so that My Shekhina will dwell among them."

A Talmudic quotation from the end of the 1st century BCE: " ...while the Children of Israel were still in Egypt, the Holy One, blessed be He, stipulated that He would liberate them from Egypt only in order that they built him a Sanctuary so that He can let His Shekhina dwell among them ... As soon as the Tabernacle was erected, the Shekhina descended and dwelt among them."

Another quotation from early 3rd century says: "On that day a thing came about which had never existed since the creation of the world. From the creation of the world and up to that hour, the Shekhina had never dwelt among the lower beings. But from the time that the Tabernacle was erected, she did dwell among them."

Although the language of the text may lead us to view "her" as a separate entity, the Shekhina is a specific way the Spirit of God is manifesting. She gives life. This is the most powerful of female attributes.

Another tradition claimed that she had always dwelt among her people, but their sins drove her, on and off, into heaven. However, she was drawn back to her children and tried to save them, over and over. This viewpoint is more in line with the New Testament idea of the Holy Spirit.

Keeping with the idea of the Shekhina returning to the people, when the Jews were exiled to

Babylonia, she transferred her seat there, and appeared alternately in two major synagogues.

Jewish tradition and teaching tells us that as the Jews dispersed throughout the world, the Shekhina comforted the poor and the suffering. She drew the sinner back to God by enlivening their spirit and conscience. She caused sinners to repent and then accepted and comforted them as if they had never sinned. Spiritually, she carried aloft the suffering and those whose hearts were broken and whose spirit was low. They were seated next to the Shekhina.. "When their spirits were healed, the Shekhina walked with them every day...."

Since we are limited in our understanding, the idea of a single entity, even a spirit, being in two places at once was disconcerting for the people. The paradox of dwelling in one place, and being other places with many people at the same time, had to be resolved.

The Talmud attempted to explain the paradox within a simple and well-known anecdote. "The Emperor said to Raban Gamaliel: 'You say that wherever ten men are assembled, the Shekhina dwells among them'."

Still, we continued to worry over the fact that God was at once in heaven and on the earth, manifesting as Shekhina. An interesting Medieval story and teaching shows the Shekhina as a total separate entity, in her most important role - interceding on behalf of her children.

Another story shows her being equated to an intercessor. "The Shekhina comes to the defense of sinful Israel by saying first to Israel: 'Be not a witness against thy neighbor without a cause' and then thereafter saying to God: 'Say not: I will do to him as he hath done to me..' "

This is obviously a conversation taking place among three distinct entities - Israel, God, and the Shekhina.

Another significant passage from the 11th century, describes Rabbi Akiva (a second century sage) saying: "When the Holy One, blessed be He, considered the deeds of the generation of Enoch and that they were spoiled and evil, *He removed Himself and His Shekhina* from their midst and ascended into the heights with blasts of trumpets..."

The Talmud reports that the Shekhina is what caused prophets to prophesy and King David to compose his Psalms. The Shekhina manifests herself as a form of joy, connected with prophecy and creativity. (Talmud Pesachim 117a)

The Shekhina is associated with the transformational spirit of God regarded as the source of prophecy:

"After that thou shalt come to the hill of God, where is the garrison of the Philistines; and it shall come to pass, when thou art come thither to the city, that thou shalt meet a band of prophets coming down from the high place with a psaltery, and a timbrel, and a pipe, and a harp, before them; and they will be prophesying.

And the spirit of the LORD will come mightily upon thee, and thou shalt prophesy with them, and shalt be turned into another man." (1 Samuel 10:5-6 JPS).

The 16th century mystic, Rabbi Isaac Luria, wrote a famous Shabbat hymn about the Shekhina or Glory of God. In it we see how this part of God is directly equated with a bride:

"I sing in hymns to enter the gates of the Field of holy apples.

A new table we prepare for Her, a lovely candelabrum sheds its light upon us.

Between right and left the Bride approaches, in holy jewels and festive garments..."

Zohar states: "One must prepare a comfortable seat with several cushions and embroidered covers, from all that is found in the house, like one who prepares a canopy for a bride. For the Shabbat is a queen and a bride. This is why the masters of the Mishna used to go out on the eve of Shabbat to receive her on the road, and used to say: '*Come, O bride, come, O bride!*' And one must sing and rejoice at the table in her honor ... one must receive the Lady with many lighted candles, many enjoyments, beautiful clothes, and a house embellished with many fine appointments ..."

The tradition of the Shekhina as the Shabbat Bride continues to this day as a powerful and moving symbol of the Sacred Feminine.

Wisdom or Sophia:
We must also look in the Old Testament, the Hebrew Bible, and consider Sophia. Her name means "Wisdom," and she is found repeatedly in scripture as the wife or consort of God.

Proverbs 8
Wisdom's Call
  1) Does not wisdom call out?
    Does not understanding raise her voice?
  2) At the highest point along the way,
    where the paths meet, she takes her stand;
  3) beside the gate leading into the city,
    at the entrance, she cries aloud:
  4) "To you, O people, I call out;
    I raise my voice to all mankind.
  5) You who are simple, gain prudence;
    you who are foolish, set your hearts on it (Wisdom).
  6) Listen, for I have trustworthy things to say;
    I open my lips to speak what is right.

7) My mouth speaks what is true,
for my lips detest wickedness.

8) All the words of my mouth are just;
none of them are crooked or perverse.

9) To the discerning all of them are right;
they are upright to those who have found knowledge.

10) Choose my instruction instead of silver,
knowledge rather than choice gold,

11) for wisdom is more precious than rubies,
and nothing you desire can compare with her.

12) "I, wisdom, dwell together with prudence;
I possess knowledge and discretion.

13) To fear the LORD is to hate evil; I hate pride and arrogance, evil behavior and perverse speech.

14) Counsel and sound judgment are mine; I have insight, I have power.

15) By me kings reign and rulers issue decrees that are just;

16) by me princes govern, and nobles—all who rule on earth.

17) I love those who love me, and those who seek me find me.

18) With me are riches and honor, enduring wealth and prosperity.

19) My fruit is better than fine gold; what I yield surpasses choice silver.

20) I walk in the way of righteousness, along the paths of justice,

21) bestowing a rich inheritance on those who love me and making their treasuries full.

22) "The LORD brought me forth as the first of his works, before his deeds of old;

23) I was formed long ages ago, at the very beginning, when the world came to be.

24) When there were no watery depths, I was given birth, when there were no springs overflowing with water;

25) before the mountains were settled in place, before the hills, I was given birth,

26) before he made the world or its fields or any of the dust of the earth.

27) I was there when he set the heavens in place, when he marked out the horizon on the face of the deep,

28) when he established the clouds above and fixed securely the fountains of the deep,

29) when he gave the sea its boundary so the waters would not overstep his command, and when he marked out the foundations of the earth.

30) Then I was constantly at his side. I was filled with delight day after day, rejoicing always in his presence,

31) rejoicing in his whole world and delighting in mankind.

32) "Now then, my children, listen to me; blessed are those who keep my ways.

33) Listen to my instruction and be wise; do not disregard it.

34) Blessed are those who listen to me, watching
daily at my doors, waiting at my doorway.
35) For those who find me find life and receive
favor from the LORD.
36) But those who fail to find me harm themselves; all who hate me love death."

Although the mainstream Christian church would forget about Sophia, the Gnostic Christians would not. In their unorthodox theology, they fought to understand the duality of the world and the Sacred Feminine. The Gnostic movement started before second century A.D., but was condemned by the emerging powers of the orthodox church and newly established church fathers. They could not control the people through Gnostic theology, which taught there was an individual transmission of knowledge from God to the individual without the help or interference of priests or church.

Most Gnostics were suppressed or killed. The last great Gnostic movement came from the Cathars. Catharism represented total opposition to the Catholic church, which they basically viewed as a large, pompous, and fraudulent organization which had lost its integrity and "sold out" for power and money in this world, a world which the Gnostics viewed as evil.

As time went on and the mainstream church became established in its power base, they could more effectively fight their enemies. The Inquisition was proof of this.

In an attempt to cleanse the world of the Gnostics once and for all, whole villages and cities were annihilated, including women and children, and even Catholics, with the justification by the church that this serious heresy must be eliminated no matter what the consequences. Arnold Aimery, the Papal Legate at the siege of Beziers, ordered his men: "Show mercy neither to order, nor to age, nor to sex....Cathar or Catholic, Kill them all... God will know his own....".

Catharism, one of the last great sects of Gnosticism, vanished from the stage of history by the end of the 14th century due to that final, fateful siege of Monsegur in 1244.

Gnostic texts were preserved and many were found in 1945 in Nag Hammadi, Egypt.

In the Gnostic text called, *The Apocryphon of John*, Sophia is quoted:

"I entered into the midst of the cage which is the prison of the body. And I spoke saying: 'He who hears, let him awake from his deep sleep.' Then Adam wept and shed tears. After he wiped away his bitter tears he asked: 'Who calls my name, and from where has this hope arose in me even while I am in the chains

of this prison?' And I (Sophia) answered: 'I am the one who carries the pure light; I am the thought of the undefiled spirit. Arise, remember, and follow your origin, which is I, and beware of the deep sleep.'"

As the myth evolved, Sophia, after animating Adam, became Eve in order to assist Adam in finding the truth. She offered it to him in the form of the fruit of the tree of knowledge. To Gnostics, this was an act of deliverance.

Other stories have Sophia becoming the serpent in order to offer Adam a way to attain the truth.

Since in the Gnostic sect of Christianity truth leads to salvation, it was Sophia, offering the knowledge of truth to Adam that symbolized salvation.

In either case, the fruit represented the hard sought truth, which was the knowledge of good and evil, and through that knowledge, Adam could become a god. Later, the serpent would become a feminine symbol of wisdom, probably owing to the connection with Sophia.

Eve, being Sophia in disguise, would become the mother and Sacred Feminine of us all. As Gnostic theology began to coalesce, Sophia would come to be considered a force or conduit of the Holy Spirit, in part due to the fact that the Holy Spirit was also considered a feminine and creative force from the Supreme God. The Gospel of Philip echoes this theology in verse six as follows:

"In the days when we were Hebrews, we were made orphans, having only our Mother. Yet when we believed in the Messiah (and became the ones of Christ), the Mother and Father both came to us."

Sophia would later equate to the Holy Spirit as she awakened the comatose soul.

So it is that within these three: Ruak – the spirit, Shikinah – the glory, and Sophia- the wisdom, that the Sacred Feminine of God is expressed.

Part Five

Understanding The Sacred Feminine

A dynamic tension between the psychological need of a feminine energy, and a hesitancy to confer or concede any control to a female exists in modern Judeo-Christian religion and culture.

Carl Jung sums up the archetypes of the female as related to the stages or evolution of man's views toward women in general. To be very clear, Jung's four stages of women are the distinct stages of evolution or maturity within the male psyche and how the man views women.

Jung believed anima or life force development has four distinct levels, which he named *Eve, Helen (who we also identify with Mary Magdalene), Mary, the mother of Jesus, and Sophia or Wisdom.* In broad terms, the entire process of life force development in a male is about the male subject opening up to emotionality. In doing so, he obtains a broader spirituality by creating a new conscious paradigm that includes the intuitive processes, creativity, and imagination and psychic sensitivity towards himself and others where it might not have existed previously. Since religion is a reflection of the collective psyche, it is very important to examine these stages and how they each influence, or have influenced, religious thought in regards to women and the place of the Sacred Feminine in Christianity.

Eve

The first is *Eve*, named after the Genesis account of Adam and Eve. It deals with the emergence of a male's object of desire. This coincides with Asherah and her place as a goddess of fertility and procreation.

Helen – Mary Magdalene

The second is *Helen or Mary Magdalene*. Helen is in allusion to Helen of Troy in Greek mythology. In this phase, women are viewed as capable of worldly success and of being self-reliant, intelligent, and insightful, even if not altogether virtuous. This second phase is meant to show a strong schism in external talents (cultivated business and conventional skills) with lacking internal qualities (inability for virtue, lacking faith or imagination).

Although Mary Magdalene was not the prostitute in the biblical account, (that person was never given a name), she did have seven demons and was not considered totally virtuous, as the apostles pointed out when they sought to dissuade Jesus from being seen with her. Speculation is that Mary Magdalene was wealthy, being from a village that was know for wealthy ship owners and fishermen, and supplied funds for Jesus' ministry. Luke 8: 1–4 states plainly that Jesus was supported by women, including Mary Magdalene, who "were helping to support Jesus and the Twelve with their own money." (NIRV)

Mary, The Mother

The third phase is *Mary*, named after the Christian theological understanding of the Virgin Mary (Jesus' mother). At this level, females can now seem to possess virtue by the perceiving male (even if in an esoteric and dogmatic way), in so much as certain activities deemed consciously non-virtuous cannot be applied to her. We will see later how the Catholic church has elevated Mary through all phases of Jungian feminine archetypes.

Sophia

The fourth and final phase of anima development is *Sophia*, named after the Greek word for wisdom. Complete integration has now occurred, which allows females to be seen and related to as particular individuals who possess both positive and negative qualities. The most important aspect of this final level is that, as the personification "Wisdom" suggests, the anima is now developed enough that no single object can fully and permanently contain the images to which it is related. Sophia means wisdom. The name of Wisdom shows up in the Old Testament as a persona, and the consort of God. In Gnostic works, Sophia was the creative force that formed the spirit of man and Sophia was Eve, who came down to offer knowledge to Adam.

When we look at these stages in detail, we notice that within each of these archetypes the church has created evolutionary stages as the body works its way back to a balance of male and female forces.

Eve

Eve – her name means "Mother of All Living, Restorer, Reviver." From Eve all human life descends. She is thus the symbol of fertility and procreation. Throughout the life of the church, women have been equated with Eve and her part in the fall of mankind in the garden. In general, the state of Eve in the male psyche has been one of deep ambivalence. There is an old saying that men hate women as a lame man hates his crutch.

Following are a few quotes from church fathers regarding women and their place in society and religion:

"Rather should the words of the Torah be burned than entrusted to a woman...Whoever teaches his daughter the Torah is like one who teaches her obscenity." ***Rabbi Eliezer***

"Do you not know that you are each an Eve? The sentence of God on this sex of yours lives in this age: the guilt must of necessity live too. You are the Devil's gateway: You are the unsealer of the forbidden tree: You are the first deserter of the divine law: You are she who persuaded him whom the devil was not valiant enough to attack. You destroyed so easily God's image, man. On account of your desertion, even the Son of God had to die." *St. Tertullian*

"What is the difference whether it is in a wife or a mother, it is still Eve, the temptress that we must beware of in any woman......I fail to see what use woman can be to man, if one excludes the function of bearing children." *St. Augustine of Hippo*

"As regards the individual nature, woman is defective and misbegotten, for the active force in the male seed tends to the production of a perfect likeness in the masculine sex; while the production of woman comes from a defect in the active force or from some material indisposition, or even from some external influence." *St. Thomas Aquinas*

"If they [women] become tired or even die, that does not matter. Let them die in childbirth, that's why they are there." *Martin Luther*

The status of women in the Bible, is disputed. Beginning with Eve herself, there is a dynamic split of position and place, owing to the fact that there are two separate accounts of her creation. The traditional church has seen the role of Eve as mother of Cain and Abel, as well as the person who was deceived into sin by Satan.

Message Bible - Genesis 1:26-28

God spoke: "Let us make human beings in our image, make them reflecting our nature so they can be responsible for the fish in the sea, the birds in the air, the cattle, and, yes, Earth itself, and every animal that moves on the face of Earth."

God created human beings; he created them godlike, reflecting God's nature. He created them male and female. God blessed them: "Prosper! Reproduce! Fill Earth! Take charge!

Be responsible for fish in the sea and birds in the air, for every living thing that moves on the face of Earth."

Genesis 2: 21-22

God put the Man into a deep sleep. As he slept he removed one of his ribs and replaced it with flesh. God then used the rib that he had taken from the Man to make Woman and presented her to the Man. **(23-25)** The Man said, "Finally! Bone of my bone, flesh of my flesh! Name her Woman for she was made from Man." Therefore a man leaves his father and mother and embraces his wife. They become one flesh. The two of them, the Man and his Wife, were naked, but they felt no shame.

In the first account, in Genesis 1:26, woman was made at the same time man was created. In the second account, in Genesis 2: 21, woman was made from man's rib. In the first account, because man and woman were created at the same time, woman was given equal status, but the prevailing ideas of the time would not allow this to stand.   It was due to this dual storyline and the fact that women were thought to be inferior to man that the myth of Lilith was born.   In this myth, Adam's first wife, Lilith sought to be his equal. The story shows this mindset was thought to be evil.

God created all things living, and then he created man. He created a man and a woman and gave them dominion over all things. God named the man Adam, and the woman He named Lilith. Both were formed from the dust of the earth and in both God breathed the breath of life. They became human souls and God endowed them with the power of speech.

Created at the same time, in the same way, there was no master, no leader, and only bickering between them. Lilith said, "I will not be below you, in life or during sex. I want the superior position". But Adam would not relent and insisted God had created him to be the head of the family and in the affairs of earth. Lilith was enraged and would not submit.

Then God communed with Adam in the cool of the evening and as he entered into His presence, Adam appealed to God. As God fellowshipped with them, they reasoned together, Adam, Lilith, and the living God. But Lilith would not listen to God or Adam. Seeing that with two people of equal authority there could be no solution, Lilith became frustrated, angry, and intractable. Finally, enraged and defiant, she pronounced the holy and ineffable name of God. Corrupt-

ing the power of the name, she flew into the air, changing form, and disappeared, soaring out of sight.

Adam stood alone, confused, praying. "Lord of the universe," he said, "The woman you gave me has run away." At once, three holy angels were dispatched to bring her back to Adam. The angels overtook Lilith as she passed over the sea, in the area where Moses would later pass through. The angels ordered Lilith to come with them in the name and by the authority of the most high God, but she refused. As her rebellion increased, she changed, becoming more and more ugly and demonic.

God spoke into Lilith's heart, saying, "You have chosen this evil path, and so shall you become evil. You are cursed from now until the end of days." Lilith spoke to the angels and said, "I have become this, created to cause sickness, to kill children, which I will never have, and to torment men." With these words, she completed her demonic transformation. Her form was that of a succubus.

Confined to the night, she was destined to roam the earth, seeking newborn babes, stealing their lives, and strangling them in their sleep. She torments men even now, causing lust and evil dreams. Her rebellious and evil spirit forever traps her. Bound in the darkness of her own heart, Lilith became the mistress and lover to legions of demons. And Adam's countenance fell and he mourned, for he had loved Lilith, and he was again alone and lonely.

God said, "It is not good for man to be alone." And the Lord God caused a deep sleep to fall on him, and he slept, and He took from Adam a rib from among *his ribs for the woman, and this rib was the origin of the woman. And He built up the flesh in its place, and created the woman. He awakened Adam out of his sleep. On awakening Adam rose on the sixth day, and God brought her to Adam, and he knew her, and said to her, "This is now bone of my bones and flesh of my flesh; she shall be called woman for she was taken from man, and she shall be called my wife; because she was taken from her husband."*

Mary Magdalene

Mary Magdalene was the woman delivered from demons by Jesus. She was a woman who was seen as deeply flawed by demonic possession. Being set free by the man, Jesus, she followed him to the end. She was a strong, committed, and determined woman, but she was a woman nonetheless. The apostles challenged Jesus because they believed he would be judged harshly by the masses for being to close to Mary. Recent discoveries have led scholars to believe Magdala, the city that Mary came from and whose name is derived from the place-name, was likely a woman of means. The city was known for its ships and fishing industry. Mary was probably part of the fishing industry and could have owned ships. Mary Magdalene was most likely bankrolling part tof he ministry of Jesus.

She was a woman who followed Jesus as he ministered and preached.

Luke 8:1-3: Afterward, Jesus journeyed from one town and village to another, preaching and proclaiming the good news of the kingdom of God. Accompanying him were the Twelve and some women who had been cured of evil spirits and infirmities, Mary, called Magdalene, from whom seven demons had gone out, Joanna, the wife of Herod's steward Chuza, Susanna, and many others who provided for them out of their resources.

She was there when Jesus was crucified.

Mark 15:40: There were also some women looking on from a distance, among whom were Mary Magdalene, and Mary, the mother of James the Less and Joses, and Salome.

Matthew 27:56: Among them was Mary Magdalene, and Mary, the mother of James and Joseph, and the mother of the sons of Zebedee.

John 19:25: But standing by the cross of Jesus were His mother, and His mother's sister, Mary, the wife of Clopas, and Mary Magdalene.

She continued to believe in Jesus after he was killed.

Mark 15:47: Mary Magdalene and Mary, the mother of Joses, were looking on to see where He was laid.

Matthew 27:61: *And Mary Magdalene was there, and the other Mary, sitting opposite the grave.*

Matthew 28:1: *Now after the Sabbath, as it began to dawn toward the first day of the week, Mary Magdalene and the other Mary came to look at the grave.*

Mark 16:1: *When the Sabbath was over, Mary Magdalene, and Mary, the mother of James, and Salome, bought spices, so that they might come and anoint Him.*

She was the first to realize and announce the resurrection of Jesus.

John 20:1: *Now, on the first day of the week, Mary Magdalene came early to the tomb, while it was still dark, and saw the stone already taken away from the tomb.*

Mark 16:9: *Now after He had risen early on the first day of the week, He first appeared to Mary Magdalene, from whom He had cast out seven demons.*

John 20:18: *Mary Magdalene came, announcing to the disciples, "I have seen the Lord," and that He had said these things to her.*

Luke 24: *But at daybreak on the first day of the week [the women] took the spices they had prepared and went to the tomb. They found the stone rolled away from the tomb; but when they entered, they did not*

find the body of the Lord Jesus. While they were puz-
zling over this, behold, two men in dazzling garments
appeared to them. They were terrified and bowed their
faces to the ground. They said to them, "Why do you
seek the living one among the dead?

He is not here, but he has been raised. Remember what
he said to you while he was still in Galilee, that the Son
of Man must be handed over to sinners and be cruci-
fied, and rise on the third day." And they remembered
his words.

Then they returned from the tomb and announced all
these things to the eleven and to all the others.

The women were Mary Magdalene, Joanna, and Mary,
the mother of James; the others who accompanied them
also told this to the apostles, but their story seemed like
nonsense and they did not believe them.

Most Gnostic Christians held to the idea of the duality of sexes playing out in multiple layers. The feminine force of Sophia becomes the feminine force of the Holy Spirit and is made the bride of God. The gender duality continues when the feminine force of the Holy Spirit inhabits the perfect man, Jesus, making him the Messiah. The gender context is ripe for the story to be continued in the persons of Jesus and Mary Magdalene, physically shadowing the spiritual relationship of the Holy Spirit and the Supreme God, as well as Jesus and the Holy Spirit.

The concept of a married Jesus is revealed in several verses of The Gospel of Philip, such as verse 118.

"There is the Son of Man and there is the son of the son of Man. The Lord is the Son of Man, and his son creates through him. God gave the Son of Man the power to create; he also gave him the ability to have children."

If one were to examine the writings of Solomon, the play on words between the masculine and feminine, and the spiritual aspects can be seen clearly. The Gnostics simply expanded on the theme.

Song of Solomon 1 (King James Version)

1 The song of songs, which is Solomon's.

2 Let him kiss me with the kisses of his mouth: for thy love is better than wine.

3 Because of the savour of thy good ointments thy name is as ointment poured forth, therefore do the virgins love thee.

4 Draw me, we will run after thee: the king hath brought me into his chambers: we will be glad and rejoice in thee, we will remember thy love more than wine.

Song of Solomon 2

16 My beloved is mine, and I am his: he feedeth among the lilies.

17 Until the day break, and the shadows flee away, turn, my beloved, and be thou like a roe or a young hart upon the mountains of Bether.

Song of Solomon 3
1 By night on my bed I sought him whom my soul loveth: I sought him, but I found him not.
2 I will rise now, and go about the city in the streets, and in the broad ways I will seek him whom my soul loveth: I sought him, but I found him not…

Song of Solomon 5
1 I am come into my garden, my sister, my spouse: I have gathered my myrrh with my spice; I have eaten my honeycomb with my honey; I have drunk my wine with my milk: eat, O friends; drink, yea, drink abundantly, O beloved.
2 I sleep, but my heart waketh: it is the voice of my beloved that knocketh, saying, Open to me, my sister, my love, my dove, my undefiled: for my head is filled with dew, and my locks with the drops of the night.
3 I have put off my coat; how shall I put it on? I have washed my feet; how shall I defile them?
4 My beloved put in his hand by the hole of the door, and my bowels were moved for him.
5 I rose up to open to my beloved; and my hands dropped with myrrh, and my fingers with sweet smelling myrrh, upon the handles of the lock.

Song of Solomon 7

1 How beautiful are thy feet with shoes, O prince's daughter! the joints of thy thighs are like jewels, the work of the hands of a cunning workman.

2 Thy navel is like a round goblet, which wanteth not liquor: thy belly is like an heap of wheat set about with lilies.

3 Thy two breasts are like two young roes that are twins.

Due to the inherent dualism of Gnosticism, sex was a symbol, and at times, a portal to a mystical experience. Many religions are replete with sexual allegories, as is Gnosticism. Proceeding from the two points of physical metaphor in Gnostic literature and the likelihood of marriage among the population of Jewish men, controversy arose when speculation began as to whether Jesus could have married. The flames of argument roared into inferno proportions when the translation of the books of Philip and Mary Magdalene were published.

"And the companion (Consort) was Mary of Magdala (Mary Magdalene). The Lord loved Mary more than all the other disciples and he kissed her often on her mouth (the text is missing here and the word "mouth" is assumed). The others saw his love for Mary and asked him: "Why do you love her more than all of us?" The Savior replied, "Why do I not love you in the same way I love her?"

The Gospel of Philip

Peter said to Mary; "Sister we know that the Savior loved you more than all other women. Tell us the words of the Savior that you remember and know, but we have not heard and do not know. Mary answered him and said; "I will tell you what He hid from you."
  The Gospel of Mary Magdalene

Mary was a sinful, damaged, redeemed, powerful person. It is the myth woven into the story of Mary Magdalene that empowers her to us. To many, she is the captive. Possessed, enslaved, caught in the midst of crime and tragedy, but at once redeemed, set free, and loved by God himself. (Mary was connected to the story of a prostitute, but this is not the case.) She is hope and triumph. She represents the power of truth and love to change the life of the lowest and most powerless of us. She is you and me in search of God.

Mary, The Mother of Jesus

The evolution of the status of Mary, the mother of Jesus, is the attempt by the collective psyche of the church to find the correct place for the feminine energies of God. However, since the church leaders have not reconciled the balance of masculine and feminine parts of God, Mary was chosen as a surrogate to be endowed with some of these qualities.

Rising to another level of the Sacred Feminine, *Ruak* becomes the female part of the Godhead that impregnated Mary to produce Jesus. The same spirit empowered Jesus by coming down in the visage of a dove. Mary was visited and carried this spirit within her womb. It is natural that she would come to be equated with the same mothering, nurturing, Sacred Feminine.

The Catholic Church was diminishing the status of women at the same time as they struggled to make sense of their own female redeemer. They began to elevate Mother Mary by announcing the doctrine of the Immaculate Conception, so errors in logic were exposed. If Mother Mary was conceived without sin in order to carry Jesus, who was conceived without sin, one must ask why wasn't it necessary for the mother of Mary to also be conceived without sin. This logic continues backward ad infinitum until Eve herself and all female offspring must be sinless. Of course, the church flatly refuses this line of reasoning, saying only that certain things must be taken on faith. This is the same tactic taken regarding the "Ever-Virginity" of Mother Mary, even in the face of scriptures proclaiming that the mother, sister, and brothers of Jesus had come to have audience with him.

It was the Greek Orthodox Church that already had the answer to this dilemma. Original sin is not in their doctrine. They state only that humans are born with a pre-disposition toward sinning. This makes the problem of sinless birth from the beginning, null.

Even though the theological events of doctrine concerning Mother Mary occurred over time, they serve as an undeniable pattern of the Catholic Church as it endeavored to "purify" women and rid them of sexuality. It is within Mary that we find the complete evolution of the Sacred Feminine, but with sexuality systematically muted and removed.

Beginning as a teenage girl, dismissed by society as a lowly female, she has, over time, been elevated to a position wherein the Catholic Church has placed her alongside, although not quite equal to, the savior himself. Some of the positions of the Catholic Church regarding Mary were not officially accepted until the mid to late nineteenth century.

In the writings of the early church fathers (Justin Martyr 165 A.D. and Irenaeus 202 A.D.), Mother Mary was seldom mentioned and only to contrast Mary's obedience with Eve's disobedience.

The doctrine of Mary as Theotokos (God-bearer) probably originated in Alexandria and was first introduced by Origen. It became common in the fourth century and accepted at the Council of Ephesus in 431 A.D.

Since the accepted Christian church continued to slip farther and farther toward the belief that sex was evil, the doctrine of the "Ever-Virginity" of Mary was established. This was the belief that Mary conceived as a virgin, but also remained a virgin even after giving birth to Jesus and thereafter, for the rest of her life. The Catholic Church rejects the idea that Mary had other children, although the Bible speaks of the brothers and sisters of Jesus. The doctrine of "virginity" was established around 359 A.D.

The doctrine of the bodily Assumption of Mary was formally developed by St. Gregory of Tours around 594 A.D. This doctrine stated that Mary, the mother of Jesus, was taken up into heaven to be seated at the side of Jesus. The idea has been present in apocryphal texts since the late fourth century. The Feast of the Assumption became widespread in the sixth century, and sermons on that occasion tended to emphasize Mary's power in heaven.

Of all the doctrines regarding Mary, the doctrine of the Immaculate Conception widened the divide between the Catholic churches and other Christian churches. This doctrine took the position that Mother Mary was born without the stain of original sin. Both Catholics and Orthodox

Christians accept this doctrine, but only the Roman Catholic Church has named it "The Immaculate Conception" and articulated it as doctrine.

Eastern Orthodox Christians reject the western doctrine of original sin, preferring instead to speak of a tendency towards sin. They believe Mary was born without sin, but so was everyone else. Mary simply never gave in to sin.

As we see in the following statement, the doctrine was not formally accepted until 1854 A.D. "The Most Blessed Virgin Mary was, from the first moment of her conception, by a singular grace and privilege of almighty God and by virtue of the merits of Jesus Christ, Savior of the human race, preserved immune from all stain of original sin."

Pope Pius IX, Ineffabilis Deus (1854)

We will examine the four Marian dogmas, among a large number of other teachings about Mary, and how they mirror the evolution of the Scared Feminine.

Perpetual Virginity – Established in the Third Century – Proclaims that Mary was a virgin before, during, and after the birth of Jesus.

Mother of God – First Council of Ephesus in 431 A.D. - Mary is truly the mother of God, because of her unity with Christ, the Son of God.

Immaculate Conception – Pope Pius IX (1854) Mary, at her conception, was preserved immaculate from the original sin

Assumption into Heaven – Pope Pius XII (1950) - Mary, having completed the course of her earthly life, was assumed body and soul into heavenly glory.

'Perpetual Virginity of Mary', means that Mary was a virgin before, during and after giving birth.

Mary was a teenage unwed mother in a world where such things brought shame and death by stoning. Beginning in the general status as Eve, stressing only her lowly station as a younger woman married to an older man for the purpose of procreation and service, she is raised by the doctrine of "Ever-Virginity" to one that is a step above the norm, being without sin when it comes to her primary purpose of procreation.

This oldest Marian dogma from the Roman Catholic, Eastern Orthodox, and Oriental Orthodox Churches affirms in their doctrine that the virginity of Mary, mother of Jesus is "real and perpetual even in the act of giving birth to the Son of God made Man." According to this doctrine, Jesus was her only biological son, whose incarnation and nativity are miraculous.

In the year 107 A.D. Ignatius of Antioch described the virginity of Mary as "hidden from the prince of this world ... loudly proclaimed, but wrought in the silence of God." The Gospel of James, a text written around 120-150 A.D., was concerned with the character and purity of Mary. The text claims that Joseph had children from a marriage previous to Mary. However, the text does not explicitly assert the doctrine of perpetual virginity. The earliest such surviving reference is Origen's *Commentary on Matthew*, where he cites the *Protoevangelium* in support.

By the fourth century, the doctrine was generally accepted. Athanasius described Mary as "Ever-Virgin".

In Thomas Aquinas' teaching, (*Summa Theologiae* III.28.2), Mary gave birth painlessly in miraculous fashion without opening of the womb and without injury to the hymen. *"From the first formulations of her faith, the Church has confessed that Jesus was conceived solely by the power of the Holy Spirit in the womb of the Virgin Mary, affirming also the corporeal aspect of this event: Jesus was conceived "by the Holy Spirit without human seed."*

Her corporal integrity was not affected by giving birth. The Church does not teach how this occurred physically, but insists that virginity during child birth is different from virginity of conception. *Pope Pius XII*

M*ystici Corporis:* "Within her virginal womb she brought into life Christ our Lord in a marvelous birth." This indicated the miraculous nature of the Virgin birth. In fact, this was the first act that would remove the stain of sex from Mary, making her a virgin forever. She is now a woman removed from the natural cause and effect of her sexuality.

Mary is truly the *Mother of God.*

Even though Mary was clear of adultery, as Joseph first thought when she announced her pregnancy, and the sin of coitus was removed from her by declaring her a perpetual virgin, when it comes to procreation, she remains a woman in service to men, being different from other women, but not reverenced. In this proclamation, the church elevates Mary to the heights of womanhood, announcing that she is "Theotokos", Mother-of-God, where she begins to be honored.

After the Church fathers found common ground on Mary's virginity before, during, and after giving birth, this was the first specifically Marian doctrine to be formally defined by the Church. The definition *Mother of God* (in Greek: Theotokos) was formally affirmed at the held at Third Ecumenical Council in Ephesus in 431 A.D. The competing view, advocated by the Patriarch of Constantinople, Nestorius of Constantinople, was that Mary should be called *Christotokos*, meaning, "Birth-giver of Christ," to restrict her role to the mother of Christ's humanity only and not his divine nature.

The holy virgin gave birth in the flesh to God united with the flesh according to hypostasis, and for that reason, we call her *Theotokos...* If anyone does not confess that Emmanuel is, in truth, God, and, therefore, that the holy virgin is *Theotokos* (for she bore, in a fleshly manner, the Word from God become flesh), let him be anathema (banned, exiled, excommunicated)."
(Cyril's third letter to Nestorius)

Immaculate Conception of Mary
Mary was conceived without original sin.

For Mary to be so different from other women, there must have been a divine intervention from the beginning. The answer was a miracle that kept Mary from the sin of being fully human, for to be fully human, according to the church, one would born as a sinful creature. This is the first doctrine to hint that the most righteous woman could be as sinless as the most righteous man, Jesus. Both were conceived without sin.

According to the Roman Catholic Church, Immaculate Conception is the conception of a child without any stain of original sin in her mother's womb: the dogma states that, from the first moment of her existence, she (Mary) was preserved by God from the sin that afflicts mankind, and that she was instead filled with Divine Grace. It is further believed that she lived a life completely free from sin. Her immaculate conception in the womb of her mother, by normal coitus (Christian tradition identifies her parents as Joachim and Anne), should not be confused with the doctrine of the virginal conception of her son, Jesus.

The feast of the Immaculate Conception, celebrated on December 8, was established in 1476 by Pope Sixtus IV. Pope Pius IX, in his constitution *Ineffabilis Deus*, on December 8, 1854, solemnly defined the Immaculate Conception as a dogma, a truth, not merely an implied condition, by the deposit of faith, and discerned by the Church under the infallible guidance of the Holy Spirit. However, the dogma is specifically and explicitly contained as an object of supernatural faith in the Public Revelation of the Deposit of Faith.

Mary is Mother of all Christians – 1579 A.D.
Obedience to God, perfect faith, and the church's position, which removed Mary from the sin that besets all who are "born of woman" has positioned Mary as the perfect mother. God has been born from her sinless body. She has raised and mothered God himself. In doing so, she has given birth to the church. Now she is given the status of the greatest mother in the world and is crowned as "Mother of all Christians." Still, as a woman and a mother and is identified only as such, she is now the zenith and apex of these things.

The Catholic Church teaches that the Virgin Mary is mother of the Church and of all its members, namely all Christians. The Catechism of the Catholic Church states:

"The Virgin Mary . . . is acknowledged and honoured as being truly the Mother of God and of the redeemer.... She is 'clearly the mother of the members of Christ' . . . since she has by her charity joined in bringing about the birth of believers in the Church, who are members of its head." "Mary, Mother of Christ, Mother of the Church."

Mary is seen as mother of all Christians because Christians are said in scripture to become spiritually part of the body of Christ and Mary born Christ in her body. Christians are adopted by Jesus as his "brothers". They therefore share with Him the Fatherhood of God and also the motherhood of Mary. To back up this stance, in the Book of John, Jesus, gives the Apostle John to Mary as her son, and gives Mary to John as his mother as he is about to die. John here, as the sole remaining Apostle remaining steadfast with Jesus, is taken to represent all loyal followers of Jesus from that time on.

Pope John Paul II , in his work, "Totus Tuus" was inspired by the writings of Saint Louis de Montfort on total consecration to the Virgin Mary, which he quoted:.

"Now, since Mary is of all creatures the one most conformed to Jesus Christ, it follows that among all devotions that which most consecrates and conforms a soul to our Lord is devotion to Mary, his Holy Mother, and that the more a soul is consecrated to her the more will it be consecrated to Jesus Christ."

Assumption of Mary

Mary was assumed into heaven with body and soul.

As time went on, the church removed women from positions of authority and spiritual leadership. The assumption of Mary in 1950 place a woman at the throne of God, beside her son, Jesus. She has surpassed being a mother and is now bodily in heaven, placing her in the company of only three others: Jesus, Elijah, and Enoch, who were also taken up to heaven in physical form.

Mary, the ever virgin, mother of God was free of original sin. The Immaculate Conception is one basis for the 1950 dogma. Another was the century old Church-wide veneration of the Virgin Mary as being assumed into heaven, which Pope Pius XII referred to in *Deiparae Virginis Mariae*. Although the assumption of Mary was only recently defined as dogma, accounts of the bodily assumption of Mary into heaven have circulated, at least, since the 5th century. The Catholic

Church itself interprets chapter 12 of the Book of Revelation as referring to it. The story appears in "The Passing of the Virgin Mary", a late 5th century work ascribed to Melito of Sardis and tells the story of the apostles being transported by white clouds to the death-bed of Mary, each from the town where he was preaching at the hour.

Theological debate about the Assumption continued until 1950 when, in the Apostolic Constitution, Munificentissimus Deus, it was defined as definitive doctrine by Pope Pius XII.

"We pronounce, declare, and define it to be a divinely revealed dogma: that the Immaculate Mother of God, the ever Virgin Mary, having completed the course of her earthly life, was assumed body and soul into heavenly glory."

Since the 1870 solemn declaration of Papal Infallibility by the Vatican I, this declaration by Pope Pius XII has been the only use of Papal Infallibility. While Pope Pius XII deliberately left open the question of whether Mary died before her Assumption, the more common teaching of the early Fathers is that she did. "

After the proclamation of the assumption of Mary, Carl Jung wrote:

"The promulgation of the new dogma of the Assumption of the Virgin Mary could, in itself, have been

sufficient reason for examining the psychological background. It is interesting to note that, among the many articles published in the Catholic and Protestant press on the declaration of the dogma, there was not one, so far as I could see, which laid anything like proper emphasis on what was undoubtedly the most powerful motive: namely the popular movement and the psychological need behind it."

Essentially, the writers of the articles were satisfied with learned considerations, dogmatic and historical, which have no bearing on the living religious process. But anyone who has followed with attention the visions of Mary which have been increasing in number over the last few decades, and has taken their psychological significance into account, might have known what was brewing.

The fact, especially, that it was largely children who had the visions might have given pause for thought, for in such cases, the collective unconscious is always at work ...One could have known for a long time that there was a deep longing in the masses for an intercessor and mediatrix who would at last take her place alongside the Holy Trinity and be received as the 'Queen of heaven and Bride at the heavenly court.' For more than a thousand years it has been taken for granted that the Mother of God dwelt there.

I consider it to be the most important religious event since the Reformation. It is a petra scandali for the unpsycholgical mind: how can such an unfounded assertion as the bodily reception of the Virgin into heaven be put forward as worthy of belief? But the method which the Pope uses in order to demonstrate the truth of the dogma makes sense to the psychological mind, because it bases itself firstly on the necessary prefigurations, and secondly on a tradition of religious assertions reaching back for more than a thousand years.

What outrages the Protestant standpoint in particular is the boundless approximation of the Deipara to the Godhead and, in consequence, the endangered supremacy of Christ, from which Protestantism will not budge. In sticking to this point it has obviously failed to consider that its hymnology is full of references to the 'heavenly bridegroom,' who is now suddenly supposed not to have a bride with equal rights. Or has, perchance, the 'bridegroom,' in true psychologistic manner, been understood as a mere metaphor?

The dogmatizing of the Assumption does not, however, according to the dogmatic view, mean that Mary has attained the status of goddess, although, as mistress of heaven and a mediator, she is functionally on a par with Christ, the King and mediator. At any rate her position satisfies a renewed hope for the fulfillment of that yearning for peace which stirs deep down in the soul, and for a resolution of the threatening tension between opposites. Everyone shares this tension and everyone experiences it in his individual form of unrest. The more unrest he has, the less he sees any possibility of getting rid of it by rational means. It is no

*wonder, therefore, that the hope, indeed, the expecta-
tion of divine intervention arises in the collective unconscious and, at the same time, in the masses. The
papal declaration has given comforting expression to
that yearning. "How could Protestantism so completely miss the point?"*
   ("The Answer to Job" by Carl Jung)

Mary as Mediatrix
   Although this position does not make her
equal to God or his son, it does acknowledge that
there is now a feminine influence and energy in
Heaven. With compassion and caring, the church
has her whispering her counsel and wisdom into
the ear of her son, the Savior.

   In Catholic teachings, Jesus Christ is the only
mediator between God and man, although priests
may intercede. He alone reconciled, through his
death on the cross, creator and creation. But this
does not exclude a secondary mediating role for
Mary. The teaching that Mary intercedes for all
believers, especially those who request her intercession through prayer, has been held in the
Church since early times, for example by
Ephraim, the Syrian "after the mediator, a mediatrix for the whole world." Intercession is something that may be done by all the heavenly saints,
but Mary is seen as having the greatest interces-
sory power. The earliest surviving recorded
prayer to Mary is the *Subtuum Praesidium*, written
in Greek around 250 A.D.

Mary has increasingly been seen as a principal dispenser of God's graces and an advocate for the people of God. She is mentioned as such in several official Church documents. Pope Pius IX used the title in the *Ineffabilis Deus Supremi Apostolatus*. In the first of his so called *Rosary Encyclicals*, (1883), Pope Leo XIII calls Our Lady, *The guardian of our peace and the dispensatrix of heavenly graces.* In his 1954 Encyclical, *Ad Caeli Reginam*, Pope Pius XII calls Mary the Mediatrix of peace.

Co-Redemptrix

This position is not doctrine, but is held as a position by many in the church. The idea was once again submitted for consideration as dogma in the late 1990's. The idea submitted by the church that Mary is Co-Redemptrix places her above all men, save one. She is now raised above those others with bodily form in heaven, except Jesus himself. At this point, Mary has been promoted.

Co-Redemptrix refers to the participation of Mary in the salvation process. Already, Irenaeus, the Church Father (Died 200 A.D.), referred to Mary as "causa salutis" [cause of our salvation], acknowledging her authority formally. It is teaching, which has been considered since the 15th century but never declared a dogma. The Roman Catholic view of Co-Redemptrix does not imply that Mary participates as equal part in the redemption of the human race, since Christ is the only redeemer. Mary herself needed redemption and was redeemed by Jesus Christ her son. Being redeemed by Christ, implies that she cannot be his equal part in the redemption process. (It seems that in this part of the doctrine Mary was born without original sin, but must have later sinned in some way in order to need redemption.)

Co-redemptrix refers to an indirect or unequal but important participation by Mary in the redemption process. She gave free consent to give life to the redeemer, to share his life, to suffer with him under the cross and to sacrifice him for the sake of the redemption of mankind. Co-redemption is not something new.

Queen of Heaven

The doctrine that the Virgin Mary has been crowned Queen of Heaven, "the Mother of the King of the universe," and the "Virgin Mother who brought forth the King of the whole world" goes back to St. Gregory Nazianzen. The Catholic Church often sees Mary as queen in heaven, bearing a crown of twelve stars in the Book of Revelation.

The evolution of the status of Mary, the Mother of Jesus has taken eighteen-hundred years to become what it is today. The king of glory now has a queen and the balance is restored in the mind of the church. But this balance is a false one and does not fulfill the reunification of the vital male and female energies in the one and only God. With Mary, there is still duality, and duality is not an acceptable answer to the unity found within one God and spirit.

Wisdom – Sophia

Sophia has a double meaning within Christian theology owing to the split within the early church between orthodoxy and Gnosticism. Wisdom within orthodox (mainstream) Christianity is presented as a spirit entity and consort of God. The book of Proverbs is a well known book of the Bible. The book of Wisdom is found in the Bibles of the Catholic Church and Orthodox Church. The verses here reflect the reverence of wisdom within the church, but they did not view her as a entity or the consort of God, even though the texts state that she is. Wisdom became directly connected with the Logos of the New Testament. Later, we will discuss the place of Sophia within lesser known sects such as the Gnostic Church.

Proverbs 8

22) The Lord created me first of all, the first of his works, long ago.

23) I was made in the very beginning, at the first, before the world began.

24) I was born before the oceans, when there were no springs of water.

25) I was born before the mountains, before the hills were set in place,

26) before God made the earth and its fields or even the first handful of soil.

27) I was there when he set the sky in place, when he stretched the horizon across the ocean,

28) when he placed the clouds in the sky, when he opened the springs of the ocean

29) and ordered the waters of the sea to rise no further than he said. I was there when he laid the earth's foundations.

30) I was beside him like an architect. I was his daily source of joy, always happy in his presence"

31) happy with the world and pleased with the human race.

32) Now, young people, listen to me. Do as I say, and you will be happy.

33) Listen to what you are taught. Be wise; do not neglect it.

34) Those who listen to me will be happy" those who stay at my door every day, waiting at the entrance to my home.

35) Those who find me find life, and the Lord will be pleased with them.

36) Those who do not find me hurt themselves; anyone who hates me loves death.

The Book of Wisdom 7
(Apocrypha and Orthodox Bible)

21) I learned things that were well known and things that had never been known before,

22) because Wisdom, who gave shape to everything that exists, was my teacher.

The Nature of Wisdom

23) The spirit of Wisdom is intelligent and holy. It is of one nature, but reveals itself in many ways. It is not made of any material substance, and it moves about freely. It is clear, clean, and confident; it cannot be harmed. It loves what is good. It is sharp and unconquerable, kind, and a friend of humanity. It is dependable and sure, and has no worries. It has power over everything, and sees everything. It penetrates every spirit that is intelligent and pure, no matter how delicate its substance may be.

24) Wisdom moves more easily than motion itself; she is so pure that she penetrates everything.

25) She is a breath of God's power a pure and radiant stream of glory from the Almighty. Nothing that is defiled can ever steal its way into Wisdom.

26) She is a reflection of eternal light, a perfect mirror of God's activity and goodness.

27) Even though Wisdom acts alone, she can do anything. She makes everything new, although she herself never changes. From generation to generation she enters the souls of holy people, and makes them God's friends and prophets.

28) There is nothing that God loves more than people who are at home with Wisdom.

29) Wisdom is more beautiful than the sun and all the constellations. She is better than light itself,

30) because night always follows day, but evil never overcomes Wisdom.

Wisdom 8

1) Her great power reaches into every part of the world, and she sets everything in useful order.

Solomon's Love for Wisdom

2) Wisdom has been my love. I courted her when I was young and wanted to make her my bride. I fell in love with her beauty.

3) She glorifies her noble origin by living with God, the Lord of all, who loves her.

4) She is familiar with God's mysteries and helps determine his course of action.

5) Is it good to have riches in this life? Nothing can make you richer than Wisdom, who makes everything function.

6) Is knowledge a useful thing to have? Nothing is better than Wisdom, who has given shape to everything that exists.

7) Do you love justice? All the virtues are the result of Wisdom's work: justice and courage, self-control and understanding. Life can offer us nothing more valuable than these.

8) Do you want to have wide experience? Wisdom knows the lessons of history and can anticipate the future. She knows how to interpret

what people say and how to solve problems. She knows the miracles that God will perform, and how the movements of history will develop.

Wisdom 9

Solomon Prays for Wisdom

1) God of my ancestors, merciful Lord, by your word you created everything.

2) By your Wisdom you made us humans to rule all creation,

3) to govern the world with holiness and righteousness, to administer justice with integrity.

4) Give me the Wisdom that sits beside your throne; give me a place among your children.

5) I am your slave, as was my mother before me. I am only human. I am not strong, and my life will be short. I have little understanding of the Law or of how to apply it.

6) Even if someone is perfect, he will be thought of as nothing without the Wisdom that comes from you.

7) You chose me over everyone else to be the king of your own people, to judge your sons and daughters.

8) You told me to build a temple on your sacred mountain, an altar in Jerusalem, the city you chose as your home. It is a copy of that temple in heaven, which you prepared at the beginning.

9) Wisdom is with you and knows your actions; she was present when you made the world. She knows what pleases you, what is right and in accordance with your commands.

10) Send her from the holy heavens, down from your glorious throne, so that she may work at my side, and I may learn what pleases you.

11) She knows and understands everything, and will guide me intelligently in what I do. Her glory will protect me.

12) Then I will judge your people fairly, and be worthy of my father's throne. My actions will be acceptable.

13) Who can ever learn the will of God?

14) Human reason is not adequate for the task, and our philosophies tend to mislead us,

15) because our mortal bodies weigh our souls down. The body is a temporary structure made of earth, a burden to the active mind.

16) All we can do is make guesses about things on earth; we must struggle to learn about things that are close to us. Who, then, can ever hope to understand heavenly things?

17) No one has ever learned your will, unless you first gave him Wisdom, and sent your holy spirit down to him.

18) In this way, people on earth have been set on the right path, have learned what pleases you, and have been kept safe by Wisdom.

Proverbs 1
Wisdom Calls

20) Listen! Wisdom is calling out in the streets and marketplaces,

21) calling loudly at the city gates and wherever people come together:

22) Foolish people! How long do you want to be foolish? How long will you enjoy making fun of knowledge? Will you never learn?

23) Listen when I reprimand you; I will give you good advice and share my knowledge with you.

24) I have been calling you, inviting you to come, but you would not listen. You paid no attention to me.

25) You have ignored all my advice and have not been willing to let me correct you.

26) So when you get into trouble, I will laugh at you. I will make fun of you when terror strikes

27) when it comes on you like a storm, bringing fierce winds of trouble, and you are in pain and misery.

28) Then you will call for wisdom, but I will not answer. You may look for me everywhere, but you will not find me.

29) You have never had any use for knowledge and have always refused to obey the Lord.

30) You have never wanted my advice or paid any attention when I corrected you.

31) So then, you will get what you deserve, and your own actions will make you sick.

32) Inexperienced people die because they reject wisdom. Stupid people are destroyed by their own lack of concern.

33) But whoever listens to me will have security. He will be safe, with no reason to be afraid.

Sophia, in Gnostic theology, is a creative, spiritual person. In one Gnostic creation story, the Archons (lesser angels) created Adam, but could not bring him to life. In other stories, Adam was formed as a type of worm, unable to attain personhood. Thus, man began as an incomplete creation. In this myth, the Archons were afraid that if Adam were fully formed, he might be more powerful than the Archons themselves. When they saw Adam was incapable of attaining the human state, their fears were put to rest, thus, they called that day the "Day of Rest."

Sophia saw Adam's horrid state and had compassion. Sophia descended to help bring Adam out of his hopeless condition. It is this story that set the stage for the emergence of the Sacred Feminine force in Gnosticism that is not seen in orthodox Christianity. Sophia brought within herself the light and power of the Supreme God. Metaphorically, within the spiritual womb of Sophia was carried the life force of the Supreme God for Adam's salvation as seen in the Gnostic text, "*The Apocryphon of John.*"

As the emerging orthodox church became more and more oppressive to women, later even labeling them "occasions of sin," the Gnostics countered by raising women to equal status with men, saying that Sophia was, in a sense, the handmaiden or wife of the Supreme God, making the soul of Adam her spiritual offspring.

Sophia represents the highest and purest attributes of the feminine energies. Sophia is intelligent, independent, powerful, creative, caring, nurturing, and a goddess in her own right. She is the consort of God.

Part Six

Searching For The Sacred Feminine in the Faces of Others

The nature and position of women are exemplified in the personages of Deborah, Abigail, Priscilla, Eunice, Phoebe, and others, whose names have been omitted from the Bible because they were simply too strong. Most women, whose stories we find in the Bible, fall into two types. They are determined, devoted and demure, or they are wayward, wanton, and wicked. There is a also a noticeable shift in the permitted positions of women between the Old Testament and New Testament.

In the Old Testament, we are more likely to find a more complete picture of the female psyche. The picture must be painted in a composite made up of several women. There are women who are like those who Solomon sees as the perfect wife. There are those who are simply wiser than their husbands, but who work behind the scenes to correct his mistakes. Then, there are those who are warriors and prophets.

We will look quickly at these three divergent types. They are the positive attributes as presented in the Old Testament. They are the faces of the Sacred Feminine exemplified in the pages of the Bible.

The ideal and perfect woman. at the time of Solomon, is summed up in Proverbs 31. She provided tireless support and devotion to her family. She was above reproach. She never defies her husband and always works in harmony with his wishes. She is the archetype of Mother Mary in the Jungian schema.

Proverbs 31:10-31
(Message Bible)
A good woman is hard to find, and worth far more than diamonds.
Her husband trusts her without reserve,
    and never has reason to regret it.
Never spiteful, she treats him generously
    all her life long.
She shops around for the best yarns and cottons,
    and enjoys knitting and sewing.
She's like a trading ship that sails to faraway places and brings back exotic surprises.
She's up before dawn, preparing breakfast
    for her family and organizing her day.
She looks over a field and buys it,
    then, with money she's put aside, plants a garden.
First thing in the morning, she dresses for work,
    rolls up her sleeves, eager to get started.
She senses the worth of her work,
    is in no hurry to call it quits for the day.
She's skilled in the crafts of home and hearth,
    diligent in homemaking.
She's quick to assist anyone in need,
    reaches out to help the poor.
She doesn't worry about her family when it snows; their winter clothes are all mended and ready to wear.

She makes her own clothing,
  and dresses in colorful linens and silks.
Her husband is greatly respected
  when he deliberates with the city fathers.
She designs gowns and sells them,
  brings the sweaters she knits to the dress shops.
Her clothes are well-made and elegant,
  and she always faces tomorrow with a smile.
When she speaks she has something worthwhile
to say, and she always says it kindly.
She keeps an eye on everyone in her household,
  and keeps them all busy and productive.
Her children respect and bless her;
  her husband joins in with words of praise:
"Many women have done wonderful things,
  but you've outclassed them all!"
Charm can mislead and beauty soon fades.
  The woman to be admired and praised
  is the woman who lives in the Fear-of-God.
Give her everything she deserves!
  Festoon her life with praises!

Now and then we see women who were wiser than there male counterparts, and act independently of them in order to save both themselves and their foolish husbands. Owning to the Gnostic belief that Mary Magdalene was given special knowledge over and above the other disciples, we will call this woman the "Mary Magdalene" of the Jungian types.

Abigail
1 Samuel 25

(Message Bible)

1) Samuel died. The whole country came to his funeral. Everyone grieved over his death, and he was buried in his hometown of Ramah. Meanwhile, David moved again, this time to the wilderness of Maon.

2-3) There was a certain man in Maon who carried on his business in the region of Carmel. He was very prosperous—three thousand sheep and a thousand goats, and it was sheep-shearing time in Carmel. The man's name was Nabal (Fool), a Calebite, and his wife's name was Abigail. The woman was intelligent and good-looking, the man brutish and mean.

4-8) David, out in the backcountry, heard that Nabal was shearing his sheep and sent ten of his young men off with these instructions: "Go to Carmel and approach Nabal. Greet him in my name, 'Peace! Life and peace to you. Peace to your household, peace to everyone here! I heard that it's sheep-shearing time. Here's the point: When your shepherds were camped near us, we didn't take advantage of them. They didn't lose a thing all the time they were with us in Carmel. Ask your young men—they'll tell you. What I'm asking is that you be generous with my men— share the feast! Give whatever your heart tells you to your servants and to me, David your son."

9-11) David's young men went and delivered his message word for word to Nabal. Nabal tore into them, "Who is this David? Who is this son of Jesse? The country is full of runaway servants these days. Do you think I'm going to take good bread and wine and meat freshly butchered for my sheepshearers and give it to men I've never laid eyes on? Who knows where they've come from?"

12-13) David's men got out of there and went back and told David what he had said. David said, "Strap on your swords!" They all strapped on their swords, David and his men, and set out, four hundred of them. Two hundred stayed behind to guard the camp.

14-17) Meanwhile, one of the young shepherds told Abigail, Nabal's wife, what had happened: "David sent messengers from the backcountry to salute our master, but he tore into them with insults. Yet these men treated us very well. They took nothing from us and didn't take advantage of us all the time we were in the fields. They formed a wall around us, protecting us day and night all the time we were out tending the sheep. Do something quickly because big trouble is ahead for our master and all of us. Nobody can talk to him. He's impossible—a real brute!"

18-19) Abigail flew into action. She took two hundred loaves of bread, two skins of wine, five sheep dressed out and ready for cooking, a bushel of roasted grain, a hundred raisin cakes, and two hundred fig cakes, and she had it all loaded on some donkeys. Then she said to her young servants, "Go ahead and pave the way for me. I'm right behind you." But she said nothing to her husband Nabal.

20-22) As she was riding her donkey, descending into a ravine, David and his men were descending from the other end, so they met there on the road. David had just said, "That sure was a waste, guarding everything this man had out in the wild so that nothing he had was lost—and now he rewards me with insults. A real slap in the face! May God do his worst to me if Nabal and every cur in his misbegotten brood aren't dead meat by morning!"

23-25) As soon as Abigail saw David, she got off her donkey and fell on her knees at his feet, her face to the ground in homage, saying, "My master, let me take the blame! Let me speak to you. Listen to what I have to say. Don't dwell on what that brute Nabal did. He acts out the meaning of his name: Nabal, Fool. Foolishness oozes from him."

25-27) I wasn't there when the young men my master sent arrived. I didn't see them. And now, my master, as God lives and as you live, God has kept you from this avenging murder—and may your enemies, all who seek my master's harm, end up like Nabal! Now take this gift that I, your servant girl, have brought to my master, and give it to the young men who follow in the steps of my master.

28-29) "Forgive my presumption! But God is at work in my master, developing a rule solid and dependable. My master fights God's battles! As

long as you live no evil will stick to you. If anyone stands in your way, if anyone tries to get you
out of the way, know this: Your God-honored life
is tightly bound in the bundle of God-protected
life; but the lives of your enemies will be hurled
aside as a stone is thrown from a sling.

30-31) "When God completes all the goodness he
has promised my master and sets you up as
prince over Israel, my master will not have this
dead weight in his heart, the guilt of an avenging
murder. And when God has worked things for
good for my master, remember me."

32-34) And David said, "Blessed be God, the God
of Israel. He sent you to meet me! And blessed
be your good sense! Bless you for keeping me
from murder and taking charge of looking out for
me. A close call! As God lives, the God of Israel
who kept me from hurting you, if you had not
come as quickly as you did, stopping me in my
tracks, by morning there would have been nothing left of Nabal but dead meat."

35) Then David accepted the gift she brought him
and said, "Return home in peace. I've heard what
you've said and I'll do what you've asked."

36-38) When Abigail got home she found Nabal
presiding over a huge banquet. He was in high
spirits—and very, very drunk. So she didn't tell
him anything of what she'd done until morning.
But in the morning, after Nabal had sobered up,
she told him the whole story. Right then and
there he had a heart attack and fell into a coma.
About ten days later God finished him off and he

died.

39-40) When David heard that Nabal was dead he said, "Blessed be God who has stood up for me against Nabal's insults, kept me from an evil act, and let Nabal's evil boomerang back on him."

Then David sent for Abigail to tell her that he wanted her for his wife. David's servants went to Abigail at Carmel with the message, "David sent us to bring you to marry him."

There is little doubt that the story below ex-emplifies "Sophia" in the Jungian types. Deborah was a prophet and judge over Israel who sensed the timing of God. She was fearless, independent, and wise. Jael was a woman who defied the ill begotten alliance between her husband, Heber, and the evil king, Jabin. Jael killed Sisera by driving a tent peg through his head and into the ground.

Deborah
Judges 4
(Message Bible)
1-3) The people of Israel kept right on doing evil in God's sight. With Ehud dead, God sold them off to Jabin, king of Canaan, who ruled from Hazor. Sisera, who lived in Harosheth Haggoyim, was the commander of his army. The people of Israel cried out to God because he had cruelly oppressed them with his nine hundred iron chariots for twenty years.
4-5) Deborah was a prophet, the wife of Lappi-

doth. She was judge over Israel at that time. She held court under Deborah's Palm between Ramah and Bethel in the hills of Ephraim. The People of Israel went to her in matters of justice.

6-7) She sent for Barak, son of Abinoam from Kedesh in Naphtali, and said to him, "It has become clear that God, the God of Israel, commands you: 'Go to Mount Tabor and prepare for battle. Take ten companies of soldiers from Naphtali and Zebulun. I'll take care of getting Sisera, the leader of Jabin's army, to the Kishon River with all his chariots and troops. And I'll make sure you win the battle'."

8) Barak said, "If you go with me, I'll go. But if you don't go with me, I won't go."

9-10) * She said, "Of course I'll go with you. But understand that with an attitude like that, there'll be no glory in it for you. *
God will use a woman's hand to take care of Sisera."

(Note: *The words between the * are not in the Septuagint.*)

Deborah got ready and went with Barak to Kedesh. Barak called Zebulun and Naphtali together at Kedesh. Ten companies of men followed him. And Deborah was with him.

11-13) It happened that Heber, the Kenite, had parted company with the other Kenites, the descendants of Hobab, Moses' in-law. He was now living at Zaanannim Oak near Kedesh. They told Sisera that Barak, son of Abinoam, had gone up to

Mount Tabor. Sisera immediately called up all his chariots to the Kishon River—nine hundred iron chariots!—along with all his troops who were with him at Harosheth Haggoyim.

14) Deborah said to Barak, "Charge! This very day God has given you victory over Sisera. Isn't God marching before you?"

Barak charged down the slopes of Mount Tabor, his ten companies following him.

15-16) God routed Sisera—all those chariots, all those troops!—before Barak. Sisera jumped out of his chariot and ran. Barak chased the chariots and troops all the way to Harosheth Haggoyim. Sisera's entire fighting force was killed—not one man left.

17-18) Meanwhile Sisera, running for his life, headed for the tent of Jael, wife of Heber, the Kenite. Jabin, king of Hazor, and Heber, the Kenite, were on good terms with one another. Jael stepped out to meet Sisera and said, "Come in, sir. Stay here with me. Don't be afraid."

So he went with her into her tent. She covered him with a blanket.

19) He said to her, "Please, a little water. I'm thirsty."

She opened a bottle of milk, gave him a drink, and then covered him up again.

20) He then said, "Stand at the tent flap. If anyone comes by and asks you, 'Is there anyone here? 'tell him, 'No, not a soul.'"

21) Then, while he was fast asleep from exhaustion, Jael, wife of Heber, took a tent peg and ham-

hammer, tiptoed toward him, and drove the tent peg through his temple and all the way into the ground.   He convulsed and died.

22) Barak arrived in pursuit of Sisera.   Jael went out to greet him. She said, "Come, I'll show you the man you're looking for." He went with her and there he was—Sisera, stretched out, dead, with a tent peg through his temple.

23-24) On that day, God subdued Jabin, king of Canaan, before the people of Israel.   The people of Israel pressed harder and harder on Jabin king of Canaan until there was nothing left of him.

In Judges 2:18, we are told God raised up judges, rulers, and leaders for the nation of Israel. This was to deliver them from the surrounding heathen nations. We are also told that God raised up the judges and God was with the judges. In Judges Chapter 4, God has chosen Deborah as judge and prophet.

Deborah calls for Barak, a mighty warrior to gather 10,000 men from the tribes of Nephthali and Zebulon. It is God's time to deliver His peo-ple from the oppression of the heathen king of Canaan. Barak presents himself before Judge Deborah and is given the strategy for victory.

An expansion of verse 8, found only in the Septuagint, places everything in perspective.

In verse 8 of Judges 4, Barak says to Deborah:

"I will go if you will go with me, and if you will not go, I will not go, for I know not the day the Lord prospers His messenger with me."

Barak is saying to Deborah, you have the timing of the Lord for this battle. There were no cell phones, radios etc. Barak needed the prophet to know when to strike the death blow to Jabin's army and Jabin's military leader, Sisera.

He was NOT a wimp. He was not hiding behind a woman. He was strong and brave; a man who led and commanded 10,000 warriors.

Even when Deborah told Barak that, a woman, Jael, would get the glory for killing Sisera, he did not flinch. What a man of character and valor. So the God plan begins. Deborah, Barak, and 10,000 mighty men camped at the river Kison.

Barak knew that Deborah had the timing of God for the battle. Deborah calls out, "Get up!!! Today is the day!" And so it was.

Sisera and the 900 chariots of iron and all the soldiers of Canaan were overthrown. Sisera fled on foot to the tent of Heber, who had a pact with Jabin to lodge or help the Canaanites who came his way. There was peace between Heber and Jabin. Sisera, we are told, was a personal friend of

Heber's.

Jael, Hebers wife, went out to meet Sisera, called him into her tent. When he asked for water she gave him milk and covered him. When he is sound asleep, Jael pounds a tent peg through his temple into the ground.

Barak was pursuing Sisera who had deserted his men and fled the scene. Jael went out to meet him and said, "Come on in. I will show you the man you're looking for."

In Judges 5, one of the most amazing victory songs in all of history is sung. Deborah and Barak sang together. Deborah, Barak, and Jael are honored. The song is a legacy to them for obedience to God regardless of who got the "glory" for the death blow to Sisera.

"And Barak said to her, 'If thou wilt go with me, I will go; and if thou wilt not go, I will not go; for I know not when the Lord prospers his messenger with me.'" This story is an excellent example of what a balance between the masculine and feminine can do when working together under God.

In any story in the Bible, one should pay particular attention to the names of the characters. They always reveal something about the personality, character, or roles played. In the above accounting,

Barak means "lightning sword"

Deborah means "to subdue, destroy, appoint, command, or declare"

Jael means "valuable, profitable, to do good"

What They Didn't Like,
They Changed

Women in the New Testament are usually glossed over. They had stations and positions; some ran churches out of their home; some were tireless workers; others were prophets. However, when the church fathers sat down to translate the New Testament, they did so in a way that diminished the perceived strengths of the women.

Here is a typical example:

Romans 16 (KJV)

1) I commend unto you Phoebe our sister, which is a servant of the church which is at Cenchrea:

2) That ye receive her in the Lord, as becometh saints, and that ye assist her in whatsoever business she hath need of you: for she hath been a succourer of many, and of myself also.

The word translated here as "servant" is rendered as the word "deacon" for men in that position. Here, Phoebe is a servant. Being a woman who was running a church, Phoebe has always been a controversial figure. Paul calls Phoebe a prostatis (translated "succourer,"). The Greek noun used of Phoebe, prostatis, means a "one standing before, a champion, leader, chief, or a protector." She stood before the people and she stood before God as being responsible for teaching and guiding those under her, both male and female.

In 1 Timothy 3:12, we read the following about Phoebe, in our English Bibles: "I commend unto you Phoebe our sister, minister [or deacon] of the church which is at Cenchrea; . . . for she hath been a ruler of many and of myself also." This is the noun form corresponding to the verb *prostatis,* translated "rule".

Let us look at the verses in context using the Amplified Bible, which attempts to clarify word meaning. Note all of the female names in the chapter.

Romans 16 (Amplified Bible)

1) Now, I introduce and commend to you our sister Phoebe, a deaconess of the church at Cenchreae,

2) That you may receive her in the Lord [with a Christian welcome], as saints (God's people) ought to receive one another. And help her in whatever matter she may require assistance from you, for she has been a helper of many including myself [shielding us from suffering].

3) Give my greetings to Prisca and Aquila, my fellow workers in Christ Jesus,

4) Who risked their lives [endangering their very necks] for my life. To them not only I, but also all the churches among the Gentiles give thanks.

5) [Remember me] also to the church [that meets] in their house. Greet my beloved Epaenetus, who was a first fruit (first convert) to Christ in Asia.

6) Greet Mary, who has worked so hard among you.

7) Remember me to Andronicus and Junias, my tribal kinsmen and once my fellow prisoners. They are men held in high esteem among the apostles, who also were in Christ before I was.

8) Remember me to Ampliatus, my beloved in the Lord.

9) Salute Urbanus, our fellow worker in Christ, and my dear Stachys.

10) Greet Apelles, that one tried and approved in Christ (the Messiah). Remember me to those who belong to the household of Aristobulus.

11) Greet my tribal kinsman, Herodion, and those in the Lord who belong to the household of Narcissus.

12) Salute those workers in the Lord, Tryphaena and Tryphosa. Greet my dear Persis, who has worked so hard in the Lord.

13) Remember me to Rufus, eminent in the Lord, also to his mother [who has been] a mother to me as well.

14) Greet Asyncritus, Phlegon, Hermes, Patrobas, Hermas, and the brethren who are with them.

15) Greet Philologus, Julia, Nereus, and his sister, and Olympas, and all the saints who are with them.

16) Greet one another with a holy (consecrated) kiss. All the churches of Christ (the Messiah) wish to be remembered to you.

17) I appeal to you, brethren, to be on your guard concerning those who create dissensions and difficulties and cause divisions, in opposition to the doctrine (the teaching) which you have been taught. [I warn you to turn aside from them, to] avoid them.

18) For such persons do not serve our Lord Christ, but their own appetites and base desires, and by ingratiating and flattering speech, they beguile the hearts of the unsuspecting and simpleminded [people].

19) For while your loyalty and obedience is known to all, so that I rejoice over you, I would have you well versed and wise as to what is good and innocent and guileless as to what is evil.

20) And the God of peace will soon crush Satan under your feet. The grace of our Lord Jesus Christ (the Messiah) be with you.

21) Timothy, my fellow worker, wishes to be remembered to you, as do Lucius and Jason and Sosipater, my tribal kinsmen.

22) I, Tertius, the writer of this letter, greet you in the Lord.

23) Gaius, who is host to me and to the whole church here, greets you. So do Erastus, the city treasurer, and our brother Quartus.

24) The grace of our Lord Jesus Christ (the Messiah) be with you all. Amen (so be it).

25) Now to Him Who is able to strengthen you in the faith which is in accordance with my Gospel and the preaching of (concerning) Jesus Christ (the Messiah), according to the revelation (the unveiling) of the mystery of the plan of redemption which was kept in silence and secret for long ages,

26) But is now disclosed and through the prophetic Scriptures is made known to all nations, according to the command of the eternal God, [to win them] to obedience to the faith,

27) To [the] only wise God be glory forevermore through Jesus Christ (the Anointed One)! Amen (so be it).

Within the above text there are certain things that stand out. The first is the true rendering of the word "deaconess" in regard to Phoebe. The second is the positional listing of certain names. Prisca, also known as Priscilla, and Aquila, for example, shows that the woman, Prisca was likely in the position of authority in the writer's mind.

In I Timothy 3: 4, 5, 12; and 5:17, Paul tells men to "rule well" their own households. These men are told to "rule" their households, as Paul tells us that Phoebe "ruled" him and many others. Phoebe held the same relation to the church at Cenchrea, that Paul says church officials should hold to their own children and household. We can see that the men should take good care of them, not "rule" them. These passages have no direct reference to rule, or government. In Titus 3:8, 14, the word is translated "maintain." This is a better rendering of the word.

Now the Apostle Paul makes use of the verb form of this word in I Timothy 5:14 (KJV), "I will that the younger women marry, bear children, guide the house (oikodespotein), give none occasion to the adversary to speak reproachfully."

The Revised Version does the word a bit more justice and translates it, "rule the household." Is Paul saying the women are the authority of the home? In these times, the women were expected to run the household. Men did not have much to do with the daily decisions of household, children, or even the domestic help, such as slaves.

In Titus 2, Paul instructs the elder women to teach the young women to be "keepers at home". The Greek word translated "keepers at home" (KJV) or "homemakers" (NKJV) is oikouros. This compound word is from oikos- house, household, family; and a guard, guardian, a watcher, a warden. We think of a warden as a masculine position of authority.

It seems that our beliefs are colored by our society. One must attempt to take away the veil of looking at the 1611 society in which the King

James' Version translators were immersed to find the truth. After the Geneva Bible and the King James' Bible were accepted as "The Word of God", other Bibles translations were expected to follow their meaning closely. Thus, many modern translators may see the truth more clearly than they can convey to the masses. Error propagates error, and the errors compound in time.

As a footnote, it is interesting to see that is Acts 18, Priscilla instructs Apollos, the man who some think wrote the book of Hebrews. It is also possible that Priscilla contributed to the book of Hebrews, but these things are never clearly mentioned in the Bible and cannot be proven until further evidence is uncovered.

At times, those translating the Bible simply chose to do away with a woman by changing their name to that of a man.

In Romans 16:7, Paul praises a woman named Junia as "outstanding among the apostles."

KJV Romans 16:7 - "Salute Andronicus and Junia, my kinsmen, and my fellow-prisoners, who are of note among the apostles, who also were in Christ before me."

Note in the King James' Version the name, Junia, is a feminine name, but she is referred to as "kinsmen". Now, look at some other translations.

Young's Literal Translation (YLT)

Romans 16:7 - "salute Andronicus and Junias, my kindred, and my fellow-captives, who are of note among the apostles, who also have been in Christ before me."

New International Reader's Version (NIRV)

Romans 16:7 - Greet Andronicus and Junias, my relatives. They have been in prison with me. They are leaders among the apostles. They became believers in Christ before I did.

Bibles and commentators generally utilize Greek New Testaments in their translation and interpretive pursuit. The Greek source documents are given names and the copies are tracked like a family tree. Both the source documents UBS4 and NA27 Greek New Testaments show *Iounian* accented with a circumflex accent over the alpha, which indicates "Junias" as being a contracted form of Junianus, a male name. Support for "Junias" is attested to by B2 , D2, and a number of minuscules dated from the 9th to 14th century.

No one translating or commenting on this verse prior to the 13th century questioned that this apostle was a woman. Before that time, most translations and copies agreed that Junia was a female who was called an apostle by Paul.

St. John Chrysostom wrote of Romans 16:7, "O how great is the devotion of this woman that she should be counted worthy of the appellation of apostle!"

Some time between the 9th and 13th century, as the church continued to oppress and diminish women, the idea of a female apostle became less tolerable and the verse was altered to fit the prevailing views of the time, an act that was done far more frequently than we would think.

Translators made up the name "Junias" to substitute for the actual name. However, the name that seemed to be the masculine form of the name they were attempting to eradicate was not a real name. No other person in any text has the name, Junias. This was an act she did not deserve. She was suffering along side the men in prison and was being tortured for the sake of the Gospel.

Early Christians under the oppression of Rome had to suffer to proclaim Jesus Christ as Lord. Junia and Andronicus, (perhaps her husband), were called apostles because they had suffered and were imprisoned.

According to Romans 16:7, Junia had become a convert of Jesus before Paul. Since Paul was converted just a few years after the Resurrection of Christ, Junia must have been one of the earliest converts to Christianity and could have been one of the founders of the church at Rome.

There was a sea-change or change of opinion in society between the times of the Old and New Testaments. The place of women in New Testament society was limited. Jesus, being often found in the company of women, was looked at as odd and skating on the raw edge of what was permissible in society at the time. As we have read the stories of women in positions of authority, you will notice that most of them (not all, but most) come from the Old Testament. The place of women in society was becoming more and more limited. Their defined place in the Christian world would become subservient and meaningless. If a woman were to attempt to assert herself, it resulted in social upheaval and her being punished or becoming an outcast.

Although the idea of women being pastors fell into the social trap, which seems so often to ensnare the truth, it is very obvious in the early days of the church, women were not only included, but were some of the first pastors. John's greeting in his second letter did not address the church as the elect or chosen lady, as some would have us believe, but instead the greeting was to a specific woman, who was shepherding a church. Yes, she was a pastor. What's more, the letter is so personal that it was addressed to her, not by the general salutation of "chosen by God", but by her name, which means "chosen by God." My name is Joseph, which means, "he shall add." Her name was Kyria, which is a feminine form of, "one who is chosen or elected by God." When rendered into an English version the name is "Electa."

Kyria, or Electra, has been swept under the rug where the church sweeps ideas they wish would go quietly into the night. Women in the priesthood? John had no problem with it.

Let's look at the modern NIV translation and then compare it to two older, more literal translations.

2 John 1
New International Version (NIV)

1) The elder,
To the lady chosen by God and to her children, whom I love in the truth—and not I only, but also all who know the truth—
2) because of the truth, which lives in us and will be with us forever:

2 John 1
Young's Literal Translation (YLT)

1) The Elder to the choice Kyria, and to her children, whom I love in truth, and not I only, but also all those having known the truth,
2)because of the truth that is remaining in us,

and with us shall be to the age,

2 John 1:5
and now I beseech thee, Kyria, not as writing to thee a new command, but which we had from the beginning, that we may love one another, (YLT)

2 John 1
Wycliffe New Testament (WYC)

1) The elder man, to the chosen lady [The elder man to the lady Electa], and to her children, which I love in truth; and not I alone, but also all men that know truth [but and all men that knew truth]...

I ask you, who are we to argue with the apostle, John?

Too Strong for the Bible

By the time texts were being selected for inclusion in the New Testament, entire books were being culled due to their disruptive messages. If books were theologically sound, but caused one to question the authority of men, it was excluded from the Bible. There was to be no contamination of the masses with foreign ideas, such as females being in positions of leadership or authority in the church or in life.

Presented here is one such book, whose theme was so disturbing that it was rejected off hand. The story of Paul and Thecla is a well known book among Bible scholars. The messages being proclaimed by "The Acts of Paul and Thecla", was one where a woman was a healer, evangelist, preacher, and leader. She was also a virgin who caused havoc by refusing to marry, deciding instead to help spread the Gospel.

The abstinence from coitus is a theme running throughout the texts, as Thecla fights to keep her virginity by refusing to marry after hearing a sermon by Paul urging purity, chastity, and abstinence. Paul urges both the unmarried person and married couples to keep themselves pure, following God, praying, and rejecting the pleasures of the world. As Paul travels, Thecla joins him in his mission, but departs from his company from time to time to teach and heal, without the assistance or permission of Paul. Time and time again Thecla or Paul upset towns folk with their messages. Over and over again Thecla or Paul were ejected from one city after another.

The story makes for interesting reading and serves as a lesson on how to be excluded from the Bible by challenging the current institutions of power and gender.

THE ACTS OF PAUL AND THECLA

Chapter I
1) When Paul went up to Iconium, after his flight from Antioch, Demas and Hermogenes became his companions, who were then full of hypocrisy.

2) But Paul, looking only at the goodness of God, did them no harm, but loved them greatly.

3) Accordingly he endeavoured to make agreeable to them all the oracles and doctrines of Christ, and the design of the Gospel of God's well-beloved Son, instructing them in the knowledge of Christ, as it was revealed to him.

4) And a certain man named Onesiphorus, hearing that Paul was come to Iconium, went out speedily to meet him, together with his wife Lec-

tra, and his sons Simmia and Xeno, to invite him to their house.

5) For Titus had given them a description of Paul's personage, they as yet not knowing him in person, but only being acquainted with his character.

6) They went in the king's highway to Lystra, and stood there waiting for him, comparing all who passed by, with that description which Titus had given them.

7) At length, they saw a man coming (namely Paul), of a low stature, bald (or shaved) on the head, crooked thighs, handsome legs, hollow-eyed; had a crooked nose; full of grace; for sometimes he appeared as a man, sometimes he had the countenance of an angel. And Paul saw Onesiphorus, and was glad.

8) And Onesiphorus said: "Hail, thou servant of the blessed God." Paul replied, "The grace of God be with thee and thy family."

9) But Demas and Hermogenes were moved with envy, and, under a show of great religion, Demas said, "And are not we also servants of the blessed God? Why didst thou not salute us?"

10) Onesiphorus replied, "Because I have not perceived in you the fruits of righteousness; nevertheless, if ye are of that sort, ye shall be welcome to my house also."

11) Then Paul went into the house of Onesiphorus, and there was great joy among the family on that account: and they employed themselves in prayer, breaking of bread, and hearing Paul

preach the word of God concerning the temperance and the resurrection, in the following manner:

12) Blessed are the pure in heart; for they shall see God.

13) Blessed are they who keep their flesh undefiled (or pure); for they shall be the temple of God.

14) Blessed are the temperate (or chaste); for God will reveal himself to them.

15) Blessed are they who abandon their secular enjoyments; for they shall be accepted of God.

16) Blessed are they who have wives, as though they had them not; for they shall be made angels of God.

17) Blessed are they who tremble at the word of God; for they shall be comforted.

18) Blessed are they who keep their baptism pure; for they shall find peace with the Father, Son, and Holy Ghost.

19) Blessed are they who pursue the wisdom (or doctrine) of Jesus Christ; for they shall be called the sons of the Most High.

20) Blessed are they who observe the instructions of Jesus Christ; for they shall dwell in eternal light.

21) Blessed are they, who for the love of Christ abandon the glories of the world; for they shall judge angels, and be placed at the right hand of Christ, and shall not suffer the bitterness of the last judgment.

22) Blessed are the bodies and souls of virgins; for they are acceptable to God, and shall not lose the reward of their virginity; for the word of their (heavenly) Father shall prove effectual to their salvation in the day of his Son, and they shall enjoy rest for evermore.

Chapter II

1) While Paul was preaching this sermon in the church which was in the house of Onesiphorus, a certain virgin, named Thecla (whose mother's name was Theoclia, and who was betrothed to a man named Thamyris) sat at a certain window in her house.

2) From whence, by the advantage of a window in the house where Paul was, she both night and day heard Paul's sermons concerning God, concerning charity, concerning faith in Christ, and concerning prayer;

3) Nor would she depart from the window, till with exceeding joy, she was subdued to the doctrines of faith.

4) At length, when she saw many women and virgins going in to Paul, she earnestly desired that she might be thought worthy to appear in his presence, and hear the word of Christ; for she had not yet seen Paul's person, but only heard his sermons, and that alone.

5) But when she would not be prevailed upon to depart from the window, her mother sent to Thamyris, who came with the greatest pleasure,

as hoping now to marry her. Accordingly he said to Theoclia, "Where is my Thecla?"

6) Theoclia replied, "Thamyris, I have something very strange to tell you; for Thecla, for the space of three days, will not move from the window not so much as to eat or drink, but is so intent on hearing the artful and delusive discourses of a certain foreigner, that I perfectly admire, Thamyris, that a young woman of her known modesty, will suffer herself to be so prevailed upon.

7) For that man has disturbed the whole city of Iconium, and even your Thecla, among others. All the women and young men flock to him to receive his doctrine; who, besides all the rest, tells them that there is but one God, who alone is to be worshipped, and that we ought to live in chastity.

8) Notwithstanding this, my daughter Thecla, like a spider's web fastened to the window, is captivated by the discourses of Paul, and attends upon them with prodigious eagerness, and vast delight; and thus, by attending on what he says, the young woman is seduced. Now then do you go, and speak to her, for she is betrothed to you."

9) Accordingly Thamyris went, and having saluted her, and taking care not to surprise her, he said, "Thecla, my spouse, why sittest thou in this melancholy posture? What strange impressions are made upon thee? Turn to Thamyris, and blush."

10) Her mother also spake to her after the same manner, and said, "Child, why dost thou sit so melancholy, and, like one astonished, makest no reply?"

11) Then they wept exceedingly: Thamyris, that he had lost his spouse; Theoclia, that she had lost her daughter; and the maids, that they had lost their mistress; and there was an universal mourning in the family.

12) But all these things made no impression upon Thecla, so as to incline her so much as to turn to them, and take notice of them; for she still regarded the discourses of Paul.

13) Then Thamyris ran forth into the street to observe who they were who went into Paul, and came out from him; and he saw two men engaged in a very warm dispute, and said to them;

14) "Sirs, what business have you here? and who is that man within, belonging to you, who deludes the minds of men, both young men and virgins, persuading them, that they ought not to marry, but continue as they are?"

15) "I promise to give you a considerable sum, if you will give me a just account of him; for I am the chief person of this city."

16) Demas and Hermogenes replied, "We cannot so exactly tell who he is; but this we know, that he deprives young men of their (intended) wives, and virgins of their (intended) husbands, by teaching, There can be no future resurrection, unless ye continue in chastity, and do not defile your flesh."

Chapter III

1) Then said Thamyris, "Come along with me to my house, and refresh yourselves." So they went to a very splendid entertainment, where there was wine in abundance, and very rich provision.

2) They were brought to a table richly spread, and made to drink plentifully by Thamyris, on account of the love he had for Thecla and his desire to marry her.

3) Then Thamyris said, "I desire ye would inform me what the doctrines of this Paul are, that I may understand them; for I am under no small concern about Thecla, seeing she so delights in that stranger's discourses, that I am in danger of losing my intended wife."

4) Then Demas and Hermogenes answered both together, and said, "Let him be brought before the governor Castillius, as one who endeavours to persuade the people into the new religion of the Christians, and he, according to the order of Caesar, will put him to death, by which means you will obtain your wife;

5) While we at the same time will teach her, that the resurrection which he speaks of is already come, and consists in our having children; and that we then arose again, when we came to the knowledge of God."

6) Thamyris having this account from them, was filled with hot resentment:

7) And rising early in the morning, he went to the house of Onesiphorus, attended by the magistrates, the jailer, and a great multitude of people with staves, and said to Paul;

8) "Thou hast perverted the city of Iconium, and among the rest, Thecla, who is betrothed to me, so that now she will not marry me. Thou shalt therefore go with us to the governor Castillius."

9) And all the multitude cried out, "Away with this imposter (magician), for he has perverted the minds of our wives, and all the people hearken to him."

Chapter IV

1) Then Thamyris standing before the governor's judgment-seat, spake with a loud voice in the following manner.

2) "O governor, I know not whence this man cometh; but he is one who teaches that matrimony is unlawful. Command him therefore to declare before you for what reason he publishes such doctrines."

3) While he was saying thus, Demas and Hermogenes whispered to Thamyris, and) said; "Say that he is a Christian, and he will presently be put to death."

4) But the governor was more deliberate, and calling to Paul, he said, "Who art thou? What dost thou teach? They seem to lay gross crimes to thy charge."

5) Paul then spake with a loud voice, saying, "As I am now called to give an account, O governor, of my doctrines, I desire your audience.

6) That God, who is a God of vengeance, and who stands in need of nothing but the salvation of his creatures, has sent me to reclaim them from their wickedness and corruptions, from all (sinful) pleasures, and from death; and to persuade them to sin no more.

7) On this account, God sent his Son Jesus Christ, whom I preach, and in whom I instruct men to place their hopes, as that person who only had such compassion on the deluded world, that it might not, O governor, be condemned, but have faith, the fear of God, the knowledge of religion, and the love of truth.

8) So that if I only teach those things which I have received by revelation from God, where is my crime?"

9) When the governor heard this, he ordered Paul to be bound, and to be put in prison till he should be more at leisure to hear him more fully.

10) But in the night, Thecla taking off her earrings, gave them to the turnkey of the prison, who then opened the doors to her, and let her in;

11) And when she made a present of a silver looking-glass to the jailer, was allowed to go into the room where Paul was; then she sat down at his feet, and heard from him the great things of God.

12) And as she perceived Paul not to be afraid of suffering, but that by divine assistance he be-

haved himself with courage, her faith so far increased that she kissed his chains.

Chapter 5

1) At length Thecla was missed, and sought for by the family and by Thamyris in every street, as though she had been lost, but one of the porter's fellow-servants told them, that she had gone out in the night-time.

2) Then they examined the porter, and he told them, that she was gone to the prison to the strange man.

3) They went, therefore, according to his direction, and there found her; and when they came out, they got a mob together, and went and told the governor all that happened.

4) Upon which he ordered Paul to be brought before his judgement seat.

5) Thecla, in the mean time, lay wallowing on the ground in the prison, in that same place where Paul had sat to teach her; upon which the governor also ordered her to be brought before his judgement-seat; which summons she received with joy, and went.

6) When Paul was brought thither, the mob with more vehemence cried out, "He is a magician, let him die."

7) Nevertheless, the governor attended with pleasure upon Paul's discourses of the holy works of Christ; and, after a council called, he summoned Thecla, and said to her, "Why do you not,

according to the law of the Iconians, marry Thamyris?"

8) She stood still, with her eyes fixed upon Paul; and finding she made no reply, Theoclia, her mother, cried out, saying, "Let the unjust creature be burnt; let her be burnt in the midst of the theatre, for refusing Thamyris, that all women may learn from her to avoid such practices."

9) Then the governor was exceedingly concerned, and ordered Paul to be whipt out of the city, and Thecla to be burnt.

10) So the governor arose, and went immediately into the theatre; and all the people went forth to see the dismal sight.

11) But Thecla, just as a lamb in the wilderness looks every way to see his shepherd, looked around for Paul;

12) And as she was looking upon the multitude, she saw the Lord Jesus in the likeness of Paul, and said to herself, Paul is come to see me in my distressed circumstances. And she fixed her eyes upon him; but he instantly ascended up to heaven, while she looked on him.

13) The young men and women brought wood and straw for the burning of Thecla; who, being brought naked to the stake, extorted tears from the governor, with surprise beholding the greatness of her beauty.

14) And when they had placed the wood in order, the people commanded her to go upon it; which she did, first making the sign of the cross.

15) Then the people set fire to the pile; though the flame was exceeding large, it did not touch her, for God took compassion on her, and caused a great eruption from the earth beneath, and a cloud from above to pour down great quantities of rain and hail;

16) Insomuch that by the rupture of the earth, very many were in great danger, and some were killed, the fire was extinguished, and Thecla was preserved.

Chapter VI

1) In the mean time Paul, together with Onesiphorus, his wife and children, was keeping a fast in a certain cave, which was in the road from Iconium to Daphne.

2) And when they had fasted for several days, the children said to Paul, "Father, we are hungry, and have not wherewithal to buy bread;" for Onesiphorus had left all his substance to follow Paul with his family.

3) Then Paul, taking off his coat, said to the boy, "Go, child, and buy bread, and bring it hither."

4) But while the boy was buying the bread, he saw his neighbour, Thecla and was surprised, and said to her, "Thecla, where are you going?"

5) She replied, "I am in pursuit of Paul, having been delivered from the flames."

6) The boy then said, "I will bring you to him, for he is under great concern on your account,

and has been in prayer and fasting these six days."

7) When Thecla came to the cave, she found Paul upon his knees praying and saying, "O holy Father, O Lord Jesus Christ, grant that the fire may not touch Thecla; but be her helper, for she is thy servant."

8) Thecla, then standing behind him, cried out in the following words: "O sovereign Lord, Creator of heaven and earth, the Father of thy beloved and holy Son, I praise thee that thou hast preserved me from the fire, to see Paul again."

9) Paul then arose, and when he saw her, said, "O God, who searchest the heart, Father of my Lord Jesus Christ, I praise thee that thou has answered my prayer."

10) And there prevailed among them in the cave an entire affection to each other; Paul, Onesiphorus, and all that were with them being filled with joy.

11) They had five loaves, some herbs, and water, and they solaced each other in reflections upon the holy works of Christ.

12) Then said Thecla to Paul, "If you be pleased with it, I will follow you withersoever you go."

13) He replied to her, "Persons are now much given to fornication, and you being handsome, I am afraid lest you should meet with greater temptation than the former, and should not withstand, but be overcome by it."

14) Thecla replied, "Grant me only the seal of Christ, and no temptation shall affect me."

15) Paul answered, "Thecla, wait with patience, and you shall receive the gift of Christ."

Chapter VII

1) Then Paul sent back Onesiphorus and his family to their own home, and taking Thecla along with him, went for Antioch;

2) And as soon as they came into the city, a certain Syrian, named Alexander, a magistrate, in the city, who had done many considerable services for the city during his magistracy, saw Thecla and fell in love with her, and endeavoured by many rich presents to engage Paul in his interest.

3) But Paul told him, "I know not the woman of whom you speak, nor does she belong to me."

4) But he, being a person of great power in Antioch, seized her in the street and kissed her; which Thecla would not bear, but looking about for Paul, cried out in a distressed loud tone, "Force me not, who am a stranger; force me not, who am a servant of God; I am one of the principal persons of Iconium, and was obliged to leave that city because I would not be married to Thamyris."

5) Then she laid hold on Alexander, tore his coat, and took his crown off his head, and made him appear ridiculous before all the people.

6) But Alexander, partly as he loved her, and partly being ashamed of what had been done, led

her to the governor, and upon her confession of what she had done, he condemned her to be thrown among the beasts.

Chapter VIII

1) Which when the people saw, they said: "The judgments passed in this city are unjust. But Thecla desired the favour of the governor, that her chastity might not be attacked, but preserved till she should be cast to the beasts."

2) The governor then inquired, "Who would entertain her?" Upon which a certain very rich widow, named Trifina, whose daughter was lately dead, desired that she might have the keeping of her; and she began to treat her in her house as her own daughter.

3) At length a day came, when the beasts were to be brought forth to be seen; and Thecla was brought to the amphitheatre, and put into a den in which was an exceeding fierce she-lion, in the presence of a multitude of spectators.

4) Trifina, without any surprise, accompanied Thecla, and the she-lion licked the feet of Thecla. The title written which denotes her crime was: "Sacrilege." Then the woman cried out, "O God, the judgments of this city are unrighteous."

5) After the beasts had been shewn, Trifina took Thecla home with her, and they went to bed; and behold, the daughter of Trifina, who was dead, appeared to her mother, and said, "Mother, let the young woman, Thecla, be reputed by you as your daughter in my stead; and desire her that

she should pray for me, that I may be translated to a state of happiness."

6) Upon which Trifina, with a mournful air, said, "My daughter Falconilla has appeared to me, and ordered me to receive you in her room; wherefore I desire, Thecla, that you would pray for my daughter, that she may be translated into a state of happiness, and to life eternal."

7) When Thecla heard this, she immediately prayed to the Lord, and said, "O Lord God of heaven and earth, Jesus Christ, thou Son of the Most High, grant that her daughter, Falconilla may live forever." Trifina hearing this groaned again, and said, "O unrighteous judgments! O unreasonable wickedness! that such a creature should (again) be cast to the beasts!"

8) On the morrow, at break of day, Alexander came to Trifina's house, and said, "The governor and the people are waiting; bring the criminal forth."

9) But Trifina ran in so violently upon him, that he was affrighted, and ran away. Trifina was one of the royal family; and she thus expressed her sorrow, and said, "Alas! I have trouble in my house on two accounts, and there is no one who will relieve me, either under the loss of my daughter, or my being able to save Thecla. But now, O Lord God, be thou the helper of Thecla thy servant."

10) While she was thus engaged, the governor sent one of his own officers to bring Thecla. Trifina took her by the hand, and, going with her,

said, "I went with Falconilla to her grave, and now must go with Thecla to the beasts."

11) When Thecla heard this, she weeping prayed, and said, "O Lord God, whom I have made my confidence and refuge, reward Trifina for her compassion to me, and preserving my chastity."

12) Upon this there was a great noise in the amphitheatre; the beasts roared, and the people cried out, "Bring in the criminal."

13) But the woman cried out, and said, "Let the whole city suffer for such crimes; and order all of us, O governor, to the same punishment. O unjust judgment! O cruel sight!"

14) Others said, "Let the whole city be destroyed for this vile action. Kill us all, O governor. O cruel sight! O unrighteous judgment."

Chapter IX

1) Then Thecla was taken out of the hand of Trifina, stripped naked, had a girdle put on, and thrown into the place appointed for fighting with the beasts: and the lions and the bears were let loose upon her.

2) But a she-lion, which was of all the most fierce, ran to Thecla, and fell down at her feet. Upon which the multitude of women shouted aloud.

3) Then a she-bear ran fiercely towards her; but the she-lion met the bear, and tore it to pieces.

4) Again, a he-lion, who had been wont to devour men, and which belonged to Alexander, ran towards her; but the she-lion encountered the he-lion, and they killed each other.

5) Then the women were under a greater concern, because the she-lion, which had helped Thecla, was dead.

6) Afterwards, they brought out many other wild beasts; but Thecla stood with her hands stretched towards heaven, and prayed; and when she had done praying, she turned about, and saw a pit of water, and said, "Now it is a proper time for me to be baptized."

7) Accordingly she threw herself into the water, and said, "In thy name, O my Lord Jesus Christ, I am this last day baptized." The women and the people seeing this, cried out, and said, "Do not throw yourself into the water." And the governor himself cried out, to think that the fish (sea-calves) were like to devour so much beauty.

8) Notwithstanding all this, Thecla threw herself into the water, in the name of our Lord Jesus Christ.

9) But the fish (sea-calves,) when they saw the lighting and fire, were killed, and swam dead upon the surface of the water, and a cloud of fire surrounded Thecla, so that as the beasts could not come near her, so the people could not see her nakedness.

10) Yet they turned other wild beasts upon her; upon which they made a very mournful outcry; and some of them scattered spikenard, oth-

ers cassia, other amomus [a sort of spikenard, or the herb of Jerusalem, or ladies-rose], others ointment; so that the quantity of ointment was large, in proportion to the number of people; and upon this all the beasts lay as though they had been fast asleep, and did not touch Thecla.

11) Whereupon Alexander said to the Governor, "I have some very terrible bulls; let us bind her to them." To which the governor, with concern, replied, "You may do what you think fit."

12) Then they put a cord round Thecla's waist, which bound also her feet, and with it tied her to the bulls, to whose privy-parts they applied red-hot irons, that so they being the more tormented, might more violently drag Thecla about, till they had killed her.

13) The bulls accordingly tore about, making a most hideous noise, but the flame which was about Thecla, burnt off the cords which were fastened to the members of the bulls, and she stood in the middle of the stage, as unconcerned as if she had not been bound.

14) But in the mean time, Trifina, who sat upon one of the benches, fainted away and died; upon which the whole city was under a very great concern.

15) And Alexander himself was afraid, and desired the governor, saying, "I entreat you, take compassion on me and the city, and release this woman, who has fought with the beasts; lest, both you and I, and the whole city be destroyed."

16) "For if Caesar should have any account of what has passed now, he will certainly immediately destroy the city, because Trifina, a person of royal extract, and a relation of his, is dead upon her seat."

17) Upon this the governor called Thecla from among the beasts to him, and said to her, "Who art thou? and what are thy circumstances, that not one of the beasts will touch thee?"

18) Thecla replied to him, "I am a servant of the living God; and as to my state, I am a believer on Jesus Christ his Son, in whom God is well pleased; and for that reason none of the beasts could touch me.

19) He alone is the way to eternal salvation, and the foundation of eternal life. He is a refuge to those who are in distress; a support to the afflicted, hope and defense to those who are hopeless; and, in a word, all those who do not believe on him, shall not live, but suffer eternal death."

20) When the governor heard these things, he ordered her clothes to be brought, and said to her, "Put on your clothes."

21) Thecla replied, "May that God who clothed me when I was naked among the beasts, in the day of judgment clothe your soul with the robe of salvation. Then she took her clothes, and put them on; and the governor immediately published an order in these words, "I release to you Thecla, the servant of God."

22) Upon which the women cried out together with a loud voice, and with one accord gave

praise unto God, and said, "There is but one God, who is the God of Thecla; the one God who hath delivered Thecla."

23) So loud were their voices that the whole city seemed to be shaken; and Trifina herself heard the glad tidings, and arose again, and ran with the multitude to meet Thecla; and embracing her, said, "Now I believe there shall be a resurrection of the dead; now I am persuaded that my daughter is alive. Come, therefore, home with me, my daughter Thecla, and I will make over all that I have to you."

24) So Thecla went with Trifina, and was entertained there a few days, teaching her the word of the Lord, whereby many young women were converted; and there was great joy in the family of Trifina.

25) But Thecla longed to see Paul, and inquired and sent everywhere to find him; and when at length she was informed that he was at Myra, in Lycia, she took with her many young men and women; and putting on a girdle, and dressing herself in the habit of a man, she went to him in Myra in Lycia, and there found Paul preaching the word of God; and she stood by him among the throng.

Chapter X

1) But it was no small surprise to Paul when he saw her and the people with her; for he imagined some fresh trial was coming upon them;

2) Which when Thecla perceived, she said to him, "I have been baptized, O Paul; for he who assists you in preaching has assisted me to baptize."

3) Then Paul took her, and led her to the house of Hermes; and Thecla related to Paul all that had befallen her in Antioch; insomuch that Paul exceedingly wondered, and all who heard were confirmed in the faith, and prayed for Trifina's happiness.

4) Then Thecla arose, and said to Paul, I am going to Iconium. Paul replied to her, "Go, and teach the word of the Lord."

5) But Trifina had sent large sums of money to Paul, and also clothing by the hands of Thecla, for the relief of the poor.

6) So Thecla went to Iconium. And when she came to the house of Onesiphorus, she fell down upon the floor where Paul had sat and preached, and mixing her tears with her prayers, she praised and glorified God in the following words:

17) "O Lord, the God of this house in which I was first enlightened by thee; O Jesus, son of the living God, who wast my helper before the governor, my helper in the fire, and my helper among the beasts; thou alone art God forever and ever. Amen."

8) Thecla now (on her return) found Thamyris dead, but her mother living. So calling her mother, she said to her, "Theoclia, my mother, is it possible for you to be brought to a belief, that there is but one Lord God, who dwells in the

heavens? If you desire great riches, God will give them to you by me; if you want your daughter again, here I am."

9) These and many other things she represented to her mother, [endeavoring] to persuade her [to her opinion]. But her mother Theoclia gave no credit to the things which were said by the martyr Thecla.

10) So that Thecla perceiving she discoursed to no purpose, signing her whole body with the sign [of the cross], left the house and went to Daphine; and when she came there, she went to the cave, where she had found Paul with Onesiphorus, and fell down on the ground; and wept before God.

11) When she departed thence, she went to Seleucia, and enlightened many in the knowledge of Christ.

12) And a bright cloud conducted her in her journey.

13) And after she had arrived at Seleucia, she went to a place out of the city, about the distance of a furlong, being afraid of the inhabitants, because they were worshippers of idols.

14) And she was led [by the cloud] into a mountain called Calamon, or Rodeon. There she abode many years, and underwent a great many grievous temptations of the devil, which she bore in a becoming manner, by the assistance which she had from Christ.

15) At length, certain gentlewomen hearing of the virgin Thecla, went to her, and were instructed by her in the oracles of God, and many of

them abandoned this world, and led a monastic life with her.

16) Hereby a good report was spread everywhere of Thecla, and she wrought several [miraculous] cures, so that all the city and adjacent countries brought their sick to that mountain, and before they came as far as the door of the cave, they were instantly cured of whatsoever distemper they had.

17) The unclean spirits were cast out, making a noise; all received their sick made whole, and glorified God, who had bestowed such power on the virgin Thecla;

18) Insomuch that the physicians of Seleucia were now of no more account, and lost all the profit of their trade, because no one regarded them; upon which they were filled with envy, and began to contrive what methods to take with this servant of Christ.

Chapter XI

1) The devil then suggested bad advice to their minds; and being on a certain day met together to consult, they reasoned among each other thus: "The virgin is a priestess of the great goddess Diana, and whatsoever she requests from her, is granted, because she is a virgin, and so is beloved by all the gods.

2) Now then let us procure some rakish fellows, and after we have made them sufficiently drunk, and given them a good sum of money, let

us order them to go and debauch this virgin, promising them, if they do it, a larger reward."

3) (For they thus concluded among themselves, that if they be able to debauch her, the gods will no more regard her, nor Diana cure the sick for her.)

4) They proceeded according to this resolution, and the fellows went to the mountain, and as fierce as lions to the cave, knocking at the door.

5) The holy martyr Thecla, relying upon the God in whom she believed, opened the door, although she was before apprized of their design, and said to them, "Young men, what is your business?"

6) They replied, "Is there any one within, whose name is Thecla?" She answered, "What would you have with her?" They said, "We have a mind to lie with her."

7) The blessed Thecla answered, "Though I am a mean old woman, I am the servant of my Lord Jesus Christ; and though you have a vile design against me, ye shall not be able to accomplish it." They replied, "It is impossible, but we must be able to do with you what we have a mind."

8) And while they were saying this, they laid hold on her by main force, and would have ravished her. Then she with the (greatest) mildness said to them, "Young men have patience, and see the glory of the Lord."

9) And while they held her, she looked up to heaven and said, "O God, most reverend to

whom none can be likened; who makest thyself glorious over thine enemies; who didst deliver me from the fire, and didst not give me up to Thamyris, didst not give me up to Alexander; who deliveredst me from the wild beasts; who didst preserve me in the deep waters; who hast everywhere been my helper, and hast glorified thy name in me;

10) Now also, deliver me from the hands of these wicked and unreasonable men, nor suffer them to debauch my chastity, which I have hitherto preserved for thy honour; for I love thee and long for thee, and worship thee, O Father, Son, and Holy Ghost, for evermore. Amen."

11) Then came a voice from heaven, saying, "Fear not, Thecla, my faithful servant, for I am with thee. Look and see the place which is opened for thee: there thy eternal abode shall be; there thou shalt receive the beatific vision."

12) The blessed Thecla observing, saw the rock opened to as large a degree as that a man might enter in; she did as she was commanded, bravely fled from the vile crew, and went into the rock, which instantly so closed, that there was not any crack visible where it had opened.

13) The men stood perfectly astonished at so prodigious a miracle, and had no power to detain the servant of God; but only, catching hold of her veil, or hood, they tore off a piece of it;

14) And even that was by the permission of God, for the confirmation of their faith who should come to see this venerable place, and to

convey blessings to those in succeeding ages, who should believe on our Lord Jesus Christ from a pure heart.

15) Thus suffered that first martyr and apostle of God, and virgin, Thecla; who came from Iconium at eighteen years of age; afterwards, partly in journeys and travels, and partly in a monastic life in the cave, she lived seventy-two years; so that she was ninety years old when the Lord translated her.

16) Thus ends her life.

17) The day which is kept sacred to her memory, is the twenty-fourth of September, to the glory of the Father, and the Son, and the Holy Ghost, now and for evermore. Amen.

Part Seven

The Resurrection of the Sacred Feminine

We have seen how the Sacred Feminine is now missing, overlooked, or suppressed in modern Christianity, a victim of translation and tyranny. We have seen how we, deep in our psyches, long for balance. This void in the church has given rise to the proliferation of New Age and Goddess worship, as well as the re-emergence of Gnosticism in the world today.

We have seen how the church has substituted figures, such as Mary, and elevated these substitutions to the heights of heaven in order to somehow fill the place of the perfect, complete, and unified God.

We have seen how the Sacred Feminine has been striped from the Bible. Through ignorance and violence, the word of God was raped, (an appropriate term considering the reason behind the assault was to diminish the place, status, and virtue of women.) In doing so, the feminine aspects of God was also removed, leaving both men and women without a full concept of what it means to be a balanced person.

No substitute of goddess, mother, consort, or lover can take the place of the pure, undefiled, complete revelation of God as a balanced picture for both men and women.

Without a heavenly template to draw upon, we struggle to find balance and unity within ourselves. Women feel oppressed and powerless. They become passive-aggressive and manipulative. Men feel superior and become brutish abusive bullies. What do we do to resurrect the Sacred Feminine? Could it be as simple as the realization and correction of the error that has been committed? Could it be as painless as a direct communion with God, the complete and whole God?

God, the father is also God, the mother. Ruak is still here. The Holy Spirit of God still resides here as our comforter. One must find it ironic that Jesus left us in a state of grace with Ruak watching over us while the church worked so feverishly to remove traces of the attributes of wisdom, nurturing and grace itself, which we consider the highest feminine aspects. Yet, they could not touch the Holy Spirit herself.

How do we recapture the knowledge of the feminine face of God? It is by a personal and deep epiphany. It is by seeing God in all facets and in all ways, not as the church teaches, but as God truly is and how God is described in the uncorrupted words of the Bible, before priests and scribes begin to change it.

There is no duality, there is only completeness. There are no male and female sides, there are only balance and wholeness for all. In God there is neither male nor female. These are illusions driven by what we see in this world. They do not exist in the spiritual realm, but there are both male and female sides to the nature of God, corresponding to our societal way of viewing these traits.

The Holy Spirit of God is still here and she is still comforting us. But she is simply that part of God we identify as female because of the attributes generally found in this earthly realm. She is not she and he is not he, God is one and whole. God is unified and complete. He nurtures us through his spirit, but the same spirit also purifies us with spiritual fire. God is here and we need to truly see what we are in God. We are the beloved children, neither girl nor boy, but simply his children, and he comforts us.

John 14: 11 (KJV)
Believe me that I am in the Father, and the Father in me: or else believe me for the very works' sake.

12) Verily, verily, I say unto you, He that believeth on me, the works that I do shall he do also; and greater works than these shall he do; because I go unto my Father.

13) And whatsoever ye shall ask in my name, that will I do, that the Father may be glorified in the Son.

14) If ye shall ask any thing in my name, I will do it.

15) If ye love me, keep my commandments.

16) And I will pray the Father, and he shall give you another Comforter, that he may abide with you for ever;

17) Even the Spirit of truth; whom the world cannot receive, because it seeth him not, neither knoweth him: but ye know him; for he dwelleth with you, and shall be in you.

18) I will not leave you comfortless: I will come to you…

25) These things have I spoken unto you, being yet present with you.

26) But the Comforter, which is the Holy Ghost, whom the Father will send in my name, he shall teach you all things, and bring all things to your remembrance, whatsoever I have said unto you.

27) Peace I leave with you, my peace I give unto you: not as the world giveth, give I unto you. Let not your heart be troubled, neither let it be afraid.

John 15:26

But when the Comforter is come, whom I will send unto you from the Father, even the Spirit of truth, which proceedeth from the Father, he shall testify of me:

27) And ye also shall bear witness, because ye have been with me from the beginning.

John 16:4

But these things have I told you, that when the time shall come, ye may remember that I told you of them. And these things I said not unto you at the beginning, because I was with you.

5) But now I go my way to him that sent me; and none of you asketh me, "Whither goest thou?"

6) But because I have said these things unto you, sorrow hath filled your heart.

7) Nevertheless, I tell you the truth; It is expedient for you that I go away: for if I go not away, the Comforter will not come unto you; but if I depart, I will send him unto you.

In the beginning the Spirit of God brooded over the earth. Now that same spirit broods over us. Like a hen to her chicks, she cares for us, exemplifying the highest aspects of the Sacred Feminine. Now we must recognize and integrate all of these aspects into ourselves, be we man or woman. A few of the attributes and aspects are revealed and demonstrated in the passages and stories of this book.

Now, it is time to ask the Spirit of God to help us remake ourselves in the real image of God, as God intended from the beginning. God is a perfect balance of both male and female attributes. God is all things good and wise, all things powerful and merciful. God is justice and compassion. God is love and strength. So should we be.

To see other books by Joseph Lumpkin visit
www.fifthestatepub.com

The Books of Enoch: A Complete Volume
Containing 1 Enoch (The Ethiopic Book of Enoch),
2 Enoch (The Slavonic Secrets of...

The Lost Books of the Bible: The Great Rejected Texts
April 1, 2009

Lost Book of Enoch : A Comprehensive
Transliteration of the Forgotten Book of the Bible
May 11, 2004

The Book of Jubilees; The Little Genesis,
The Apocalypse of Moses
February 1, 2006

Fallen Angels, the Watchers, and the
Origins of Evil
February 20, 2006

The Encyclopedia of Lost and Rejected Scriptures:
The Pseudepigrapha and Apocrypha
February 9, 2010

Banned From The Bible: Books Banned, Rejected,
and Forbidden
September 4, 2008

The Apocrypha: Including Books from
the Ethiopic Bible
May 17, 2009

The Gospel Of Thomas
July 19, 2005

The First and Second Books of Adam and Eve:
The Conflict With Satan
February 3, 2009

The Lost Books of the New Testament
November 26, 2008

The Gnostic Gospels of Philip,
Mary Magdalene, and Thomas
January 1, 2008

CPSIA information can be obtained
at www.ICGtesting.com
Printed in the USA
BVHW040219030119
536952BV00020B/489/P

9 781936 533138